Dreams That Turn
Over a Page

GW00771965

In *Dreams That Turn Over a Page*, Jean-Michel Quinodoz discusses a particular type of dream that comes after a phase in analysis where integration has taken place. Accompanied by anxiety and fear, which seem surprising as the dream follows a phase of integrative work in the analysis, these dreams are in fact a mark of progression as they indicate a capacity to own anxiety.

Quinodoz describes the important technical implications of this understanding, suggesting that it is essential to interpret to the patient that the anxiety indicates not a regression, but a shift in the opposite direction. In addition to the theory and discussion of the literature, he gives many clinical examples of such dreams from patients in psychoanalysis to illustrate the concepts of dreams that turn over a page. As Freud's classical theory of dreams does not by itself suffice to interpret or explain the formation of these particular dreams, Quinodoz invokes contemporary ideas to understand the underlying transformations which bring the 'return' of split-off parts of the self during the phases of integration.

The author considers the reasons why dreams that mark this transition have a more powerful impact than others on both patient and analyst, and observes similarities between the clinical impact of such a dream and the aesthetic impact of a work of art.

Jean-Michel Quinodoz is a psychoanalyst in private practice in Geneva. He is a Training Analyst of the Swiss Psychoanalytical Society and is the author of *The Taming of Solitude: Separation Anxiety in Psychoanalysis*. He is also Editor for Europe of the *International Journal of Psycho-Analysis*.

THE NEW LIBRARY OF PSYCHOANALYSIS

The New Library of Psychoanalysis was launched in 1987 in association with the Institute of Psycho-Analysis, London. Its purpose is to facilitate a greater and more widespread appreciation of what psychoanalysis is really about and to provide a forum for increasing mutual understanding between psychoanalysts and those working in other disciplines such as history, linguistics, literature, medicine, philosophy, psychology and the social sciences. It is intended that the titles selected for publication in the series should deepen and develop psychoanalytic thinking and technique, contribute to psychoanalysis from outside, or contribute to other disciplines from a psychoanalytical perspective.

The Institute, together with the British Psycho-Analytical Society, runs a low-fee psychoanalytic clinic, organizes lectures and scientific events concerned with psychoanalysis and publishes the *International Journal of Psycho-Analysis*. It also runs the only UK training course in psychoanalysis which leads to membership of the International Psychoanalytical Association – the body which preserves internationally agreed standards of training, of professional entry, and of professional ethics and practice for psychoanalysis as initiated and developed by Sigmund Freud. Distinguished members of the Institute have included Michael Balint, Wilfred Bion, Ronald Fairbairn, Anna Freud, Ernest Jones, Melanie Klein, John Rickman and Donald Winnicott.

Volumes 1–11 in the series were prepared under the general editorship of David Tuckett. Volumes 12–39 appeared under the general editorship of Elizabeth Bott Spillius. Volumes 40–42 were under the general editorship of Susan Budd. This volume is under the general editorship of Dana Birksted-Breen. Ronald Britton, Eglé Laufer, Donald Campbell, Michael Parsons, Rosine Jozef Perelberg, David Taylor and Stephen Grosz have acted as associate editors for various periods.

ALSO IN THIS SERIES

1 *Impasse and Interpretation* Herbert Rosenfeld
2 *Psychoanalysis and Discourse* Patrick Mahoney
3 *The Suppressed Madness of Sane Men* Marion Milner
4 *The Riddle of Freud* Estelle Roith
5 *Thinking, Feeling, and Being* Ignacio Matte-Blanco
6 *The Theatre of the Dream* Salomon Resnik
7 *Melanie Klein Today: Volume 1, Mainly Theory* Edited by Elizabeth Bott Spillius
8 *Melanie Klein Today: Volume 2, Mainly Practice* Edited by Elizabeth Bott Spillius
9 *Psychic Equilibrium and Psychic Change: Selected Papers of Betty Joseph* Edited by Michael Feldman and Elizabeth Bott Spillius
10 *About Children and Children-No-Longer: Collected Papers 1942–80* Paula Heimann. Edited by Margret Tonnesmann
11 *The Freud–Klein Controversies 1941–45* Edited by Pearl King and Riccardo Steiner
12 *Dream, Phantasy and Art* Hanna Segal
13 *Psychic Experience and Problems of Technique* Harold Stewart
14 *Clinical Lectures on Klein & Bion* Edited by Robin Anderson
15 *From Fetus to Child* Alessandra Piontelli
16 *A Psychoanalytic Theory of Infantile Experience: Conceptual and Clinical Reflections* E. Gaddini. Edited by Adam Limentani
17 *The Dream Discourse Today* Edited and introduced by Sara Flanders
18 *The Gender Conundrum: Contemporary Psychoanalytic Perspectives on Femininity and Masculinity* Edited and introduced by Dana Breen
19 *Psychic Retreats* John Steiner
20 *The Taming of Solitude: Separation Anxiety in Psychoanalysis* Jean-Michel Quinodoz
21 *Unconscious Logic: An Introduction to Matte Blanco's Bi-logic and its Uses* Eric Rayner
22 *Understanding Mental Objects* Meir Perlow
23 *Life, Sex and Death: Selected Writings of William Gillespie* Edited and introduced by Michael Sinason
24 *What Do Psychoanalysts Want?: The Problem of Aims in Psychoanalytic Therapy* Joseph Sandler and Anna Ursula Dreher
25 *Michael Balint: Object Relations, Pure and Applied* Harold Stewart
26 *Hope: A Shield in the Economy of Borderline States* Anna Potamianou
27 *Psychoanalysis, Literature & War: Papers 1972–1995* Hanna Segal
28 *Emotional Vertigo: Between Anxiety and Pleasure* Danielle Quinodoz
29 *Early Freud and Late Freud* Ilse Grubrich-Simitis
30 *A History of Child Psychoanalysis* Claudine and Pierre Geissmann
31 *Belief and Imagination: Explorations in Psychoanalysis* Ronald Britton

32 *A Mind of One's Own: A Kleinian View of Self and Object* Robert A. Caper
33 *Psychoanalytic Understanding of Violence and Suicide* Edited by Rosine Jozef Perelberg
34 *On Bearing Unbearable States of Mind* Ruth Riesenberg-Malcolm
35 *Psychoanalysis on the Move: The Work of Joseph Sandler* Edited by Peter Fonagy, Arnold M. Cooper and Robert S. Wallerstein
36 *The Dead Mother: The Work of André Green* Edited by Gregorio Kohon
37 *The Fabric of Affect in the Psychoanalytic Discourse* André Green
38 *The Bi-Personal Field: Experiences of Child Analysis* Antonino Ferro
39 *The Dove that Returns, the Dove that Vanishes: Paradox and Creativity in Psychoanalysis* Michael Parsons
40 *Ordinary People, Extra-ordinary Protections: A Post Kleinian Approach to the Treatment of Primitive Mental States* Judith Mitrani
41 *The Violence of Interpretation: From Pictogram to Statement* Piera Aulagnier. Translated by Alan Sheridan
42 *The Importance of Fathers* Judith Trowell and Alicia Etchegoyen

THE NEW LIBRARY OF PSYCHOANALYSIS

43

General Editor: Dana Birksted-Breen

Dreams That Turn Over a Page

Paradoxical Dreams in Psychoanalysis

Jean-Michel Quinodoz

Foreword by Hanna Segal
Translated by Philip Slotkin

First published as *Les rêves qui tournent une page*,
Presses Universitaires de France, 2001

BRUNNER-ROUTLEDGE
ALERE FLAMMAM
Taylor & Francis Group

English language edition first published 2002
by Brunner-Routledge
27 Church Road, Hove, East Sussex BN3 2FA

Simultaneously published in the USA and Canada
by Taylor & Francis Inc
29 West 35th Street, New York, NY 10001

Brunner-Routledge is an imprint of the Taylor & Francis Group

Typeset in Bembo by
Keystroke, Jacaranda Lodge, Wolverhampton
Printed and bound in Great Britain by
Biddles Ltd, Guildford and King's Lynn

British Library Cataloguing in Publication Data
A catalogue record for this book is available from the British Library

Library of Congress Cataloging in Publication Data
A catalogue record for this book has been requested

ISBN 1–58391–264–9 (hbk)
ISBN 1–58391-265–7 (pbk)

Contents

Acknowledgements   xi
Foreword by Hanna Segal   xiii

Part One: Clinical characteristics   1

1   What are dreams that turn over a page?   3
     A subject with clearly defined boundaries   3
     Paradoxical dreams   3
     Other types of dream also indicate better integration   6
     The fruit of experience   6
     The sense of a metaphor   8

2   A source of uncanny feelings and anxiety   9
     Anxiety, manifest content and latent content   9
     Hope and anxiety   9
     Dream or nightmare?   10
     Uncanny (*unheimlich*) affects and affects of anxiety   10
     The uncanny: The 'return' of the repressed and the 'return' of the
       split-off?   11
     The return of projected parts and the consequent threat to the
       cohesion of the ego   12
     The affect of helplessness and the presence of the psychoanalyst   13

3   Countertransference and containing capacity   14
     For the psychoanalyst   14
     A clinical example: Albert's dream   16

Contents

4 Progress and retreat in response to progress   20
    Reversal of the classical sequence 20
    Dream formation in the context of the transference 21
    Integration and working through of separation anxieties 21
    Criteria for evaluating progress and integration 22
    Progress and retreat in response to progress and regression 23
    Recurrence of ambivalence 24
    Ambivalence and the negative therapeutic reaction 25

5 Retrospective illumination   26
    Direct access to the unconscious 'program'? 26
    The role of unconscious fantasy 26
    Unconscious fantasy, drives, defences and personality structure 27
    Similarity to 'recapitulative dreams' 28
    Emergence of unconscious homosexual tendencies 28

Part Two: Interpretations   31

6 Interpreting in two stages   33
    Why two stages? 33
    First stage of interpretation 34
    Second stage of interpretation 37

7 Interpretations of a dream that turns over a page:
    Tania's dream   40
    Unconscious motivation of a request for analysis 40
    Risk of impasse 42
    Dawning of consciousness of the transference conflicts 43
    A dream that turns over a page 46
    Transformations in Tania's dreams 51

Part Three: Dreams and integration   53

8 Investigations in the psychoanalytic literature   55
    Similar but different dreams 55
    Dreams, anxiety and splitting of the ego in Freud 56
    Post-Freudian contributions 58

9 Classical and post-Freudian approaches   69
    The classical approach, its developments and limits 69
    Post-Freudian contributions to dream theory 73

Contents

10 Formation of dreams that turn over a page: Hypotheses   77
    The wish for integration and its expression in dreams 77
    Dreams as an expression of the conflict between the life and
      death drives 82
    The negative therapeutic reaction and dreams that turn over
      a page 84

11 Impact: Clinical and aesthetic   87
    Clinical impact of dreams that turn over a page 87
    Aesthetic impact of dreams that turn over a page 89
    Conclusions 96

Bibliography   98
Author index   103
Subject index   104

Acknowledgements

I would like to thank Hanna Segal for her Foreword and for her stimulating teaching, especially when she came regularly to Geneva. I had very helpful discussions of my ideas with many colleagues. I particularly wish to thank Dana Birksted-Breen, editor of the New Library of Psychoanalysis, André Haynal and Paco Palacio, who read the whole manuscript, for their invaluable comments. Special thanks go to Philip Slotkin for his wonderful translation from French into English. My wife Danielle has contributed by her loving patience and her constructive criticisms. Finally, I want to thank the Research Advisory Board of the International Psychoanalytical Association for the grant which supported this clinical investigation on dreams and the translation of this book into English.

Foreword

Jean-Michel Quinodoz is the author of *The Taming of Solitude* (1991). In that book he addresses himself to an important aspect of ending an analysis. He describes how, towards the end of treatment and concurrently with and succeeding the mourning processes, one can observe an uplift – often felt by the patient as a pleasurable sensation of managing to 'fly with his own wings': 'It is a new and complex sensation, in which joy mingles with a little fear' (ibid.: 172). This can easily be interpreted as a manic defence. In Quinodoz's view this phenomenon isn't defensive but more a positive outcome of the mourning process, resulting from the patient having established a good internal object as a source of added strength and inspiration. Quinodoz calls it *portance* (translated from French as 'buoyancy'), which is a force providing both the strength of an arch or of a foundation and the lift of a plane. Over-interpreting the manic aspect predominantly would be felt by the patient as attacking his and the analytical achievement. In the process of analysing this phenomenon Quinodoz examines minutely the shift from the paranoid-schizoid to the depressive position (PS ↔ D) and the meaning of the elaboration of the depressive position.

The present book has a similar inspiration – the care not to view a positive development, which at first sight appears to be pathological, as a regression and negative therapeutic reaction. Quinodoz considers a category of dreams, which he describes as *les rêves qui tournent une page*. The dreams he describes appear at a time when an analysis is going well. There is a feeling of a good relationship between analyst and patient and constructive work is being done. Suddenly, to the great dismay of the patient, a dream appears, revealing a very primitive and regressed state of mind. It is characteristic of such dreams that when the patient awakes he is profoundly shaken and frightened, feeling that the analytic progress is an illusion, that he is 'back where he started'. All hope is lost and often there is a fear of going mad.

The analyst himself may be shaken and profoundly affected in the counter-transference, seeing the patient's dream and his state of mind, and he may himself be infected by the patient's despair. However, if the analyst does not succumb to this powerful projection he can view it from a different angle. He can consider that the patient's ego is sufficiently strengthened and his trust in the analyst strong enough to bring into the analysis deeper levels of hitherto split-off psychotic parts.

Quinodoz sees these dreams as a further step towards integration, with all the anxieties that it involves. If the analyst can tolerate the initial assault of this material and work it through with the patient, pointing out the positive aspect as well as the anxieties, the patient loses his horror and can use the dream and see it as a further step in integration. Such dreams, according to Quinodoz, are pivotal in the analysis and patients frequently refer to them later as a turning point.

This book continues and develops Quinodoz's original approach and it fits in well with modern Kleinian developments. For instance, Britton (1998: 69), in a chapter called 'Before and after the depressive position', addresses himself to the problem of the PS $\leftrightarrow$ D transition. Klein made the point that the depressive position is never achieved once and for all, and that, throughout life, there are fluctuations between the two. It is not static but a constant to and fro (PS $\leftrightarrow$ D). Britton, following also Bion in that area, emphasizes that this to and fro is not just progress and unavoidable regression but that the move back is in itself part of the growing process. It is a *reculer pour mieux sauter*. We have to regress to integrate more, otherwise development comes to a stop. 'Yesterday's depressive position becomes tomorrow's defensive organization' (ibid.: 73).

Quinodoz describes how this applies to the realm of dreams. Both Quinodoz and Britton differentiate between malignant regression (for Britton it is a regression to a previous psychotic defensive organization) and a going back to face psychotic anxieties again and achieve a higher and richer level of integration. But the analyst's life is never easy, because usually they coexist and it is the analyst's task to see these structures in the whole context of the analysis at that point. He has to be aware of the function that the recounting of the dream plays in the session and of the degree of symbolization and elaboration, as against massive evacuation. He must see the function of the dream in the session in both the patient's and his own mind, because the analyst's response can affect the function, which often changes during the session, and the analyst's response may affect this in a negative or positive way. Quinodoz is wise to warn us about that.

Hanna Segal
March 2001

PART ONE

Clinical characteristics

1

What are dreams that turn over a page?

A subject with clearly defined boundaries

I wrote this book to draw attention to a particular kind of dream I have regularly observed both in my own analysands and in supervisions, which I have called 'dreams that turn over a page' (J.-M. Quinodoz 1987, 1999, 2000b). My ideas on this clearly defined subject are based mainly on the psychoanalytic theory of dream interpretation as established by Freud (1900a), as well as on the developments of the post-Freudian psychoanalysts. Although I concentrate on a particular type of dream, my references to contemporary contributions broaden the scope of my subject-matter; however, it is not my intention to provide an exhaustive review of the present-day psychoanalytic position on the interpretation of dreams.

Paradoxical dreams

The characteristic feature of these dreams is that they include an anxiety-inducing primitive manifest content that frightens the dreamer, whereas for the psychoanalyst, notwithstanding their regressive appearance, they signify the completion of a stage in the processes of psychic integration. This characteristic has decisive technical consequences. After all, because the content of these dreams is regressive, although they paradoxically correspond to a phase of integration, the psychoanalyst may be induced to consider their regressive aspect only, disregarding the context of progress in the analysand's psychic processes; in this case he[1] is liable to interpret the content of these dreams in isolation,

---

1 [Translator's note: To avoid clumsy constructions, where applicable the masculine personal pronoun and possessive adjective are used throughout for both sexes.]

thereby encouraging regression. It therefore seemed to me essential for psychoanalysts to be able to identify dreams of this kind and to distinguish them from
other common dreams, so that they can be interpreted in the appropriate
context, namely that of a better integration of psychic life.

Another important characteristic of dreams that turn over a page is that their
regressive content is closely bound up with changes observed in the psychic
processes governing the analysand's transference in the immediately preceding
period. Indeed, such dreams often surprise the psychoanalyst because they reveal
with unusual clarity and coherence the structure of the unconscious fantasies
underlying the dreamer's intrapsychic conflicts just when, paradoxically, these
conflicts are in the process of being overcome. In other words, these dreams
bring out crucial aspects of the 'primal fantasy matrix' (Perron-Borelli & Perron
1987), which had remained unconscious not only to the patient but also to the
analyst until it appeared in a dream: 'It is rather like suddenly being presented
with the program underlying the data that normally constitutes the whole of
the on-screen display' (J.-M. Quinodoz 1987: 837).

Besides this aspect, dreams that turn over a page have another paradoxical
characteristic. In classical technique, the psychoanalyst begins by analysing the
unconscious resistances due to repression – in particular, those whose representations arise in dreams – and change occurs at a second stage when these
resistances are worked through. In the particular type of dream described here,
the opposite is the case: the psychoanalyst first notices a change in the patient's
psychic processes and is then surprised, at a second stage, by the appearance
of a significant dream whose content retrospectively casts light on the nature of
the change observed and sets the process of working through in motion again.
Such dreams thus perform a function of working through in that they illuminate
after the event a change in which the components of the underlying fantasy
constellation had not hitherto emerged: 'Paradoxically, nothing of the newly
acquired internal situation appears in such dreams; *all that can be discerned is the
regressive internal situation that has just been abandoned*' (ibid.).

It was because of the working-through function of dreams of this type
that I first described them as 'dreams that turn over *the* page' (J.-M. Quinodoz
1987). I later amended this appellation to 'dreams that turn over *a* page' (J.-M.
Quinodoz 1999), which I considered more appropriate because such dreams
may occur not just once, as the original term might have suggested, but repeatedly
and at any point in the psychoanalytic process.

Three short examples

The following three short examples of dreams that turn over a page will serve
as an introduction to illustrate the basis of their paradoxical character.

One of my female analysands systematically arrived late for her four weekly
sessions and would always leave the door of the waiting room open behind her.

4

My attempts to interpret the unconscious transference reasons for this claus-trophobic symptom had remained fruitless. One day, however, quite out of the blue, the patient began to come punctually and to close the waiting room door. She made no comment about this change, which was nevertheless significant, and which surprised me. A few sessions later, she brought a dream that had filled her with anxiety and whose manifest content had made her think that she would stay mad all her life: she had dreamed that she was being locked up in a prison from which she would never emerge. So it was after the patient had taken the step of overcoming her claustrophobic symptom in the transference relationship that she paradoxically produced a dream of claustrophobic anxiety. How can this be accounted for?

My second example concerns a male analysand who was afraid of committing himself to an affective relationship on account of his anxiety at the idea that if someone became important in his life, he would run the risk of losing that person and having to face the pain of separation. This inhibition had been reproduced with me in the form of a difficulty in fully committing himself to the transference relationship, but it gradually diminished with the progress of our analysis of his difficulty in working through affects of mourning. This change was also reflected in his daily life; for example, he told me that he had tidied up his house, sorted out the things he wanted to keep, got rid of a lot of accumulated rubbish, and sent off some important letters that had been waiting for some time to be dealt with. He had imagined for the first time, too, that he would have to fix a date for ending his analysis. One day he dreamed with intense anxiety that he had to catch a train but was unable to get into the carriage, and that he had to take a lift but could not get through the door: 'I mess everything up! I shall never get anywhere! As you can see, I am not making any progress!' In view of the context, I interpreted to him that, just when he was succeeding in making choices and confronting situations of separation, he had managed to represent to himself in a dream a situation that portrayed his difficulty in committing himself to me – getting into a train or lift – and showed how strongly he felt that he would never succeed in doing so, and in particular in ever leaving me. With the ensuing diminution of his anxiety, he was able to perceive the unconscious sexual symbolism of his inhibitions – in particular, the thought of 'introducing himself' into a relationship – to become conscious of his ambivalence and to work through not only his separation anxieties but also his castration anxieties at various levels.

Finally, here is another brief example. I once had a female patient who, for a long time in her analysis, was so 'stuck' to my breast in a fantasy of fusion that everything she perceived both inside and outside herself seemed to her to be blurred and indistinct. On emerging from this narcissistic relationship and beginning to see me as a separate person independent of herself – that is, on ceasing to be symbolically so firmly 'stuck' to my breast – this patient had an anxiety dream in which her vision was clouded because she was wearing spectacles with opaque lenses like magnifying glasses. She said: 'It felt as if I was forced to stick my nose up against you, and even then I could not see you.' The patient was thus using a troubling dream to represent to herself the blurred nature of her former perception of me, just when, paradoxically, she had succeeded in perceiving me as a whole person.

I have presented these three dreams in the form of a brief outline and out of context, solely to illustrate provisionally some of the main characteristics of their type. Each of these dreams exhibits a regressive manifest content that frightens the dreamer, whereas the psychoanalyst may see them as a way of representing the difficulties in the process of being worked through, corresponding to a phase of progress and integration. It is this paradox that makes it important for the psychoanalyst to be technically capable of identifying such dreams, so that he can interpret them as a sign of better psychic integration. The patient can then work through them in a progressive context instead of experiencing them as betokening a worrying step back.

Other types of dream also indicate better integration

Dreams that turn over a page are not the only ones that tell of progress in the psychoanalytic process. However, these other dreams are different; they lack the characteristics of the ones described in this book, and are easier to recognize as signs of greater psychic integration.

For instance, if a male patient dreams of women for the first time, having previously only had dreams featuring men, both the dreamer and the analyst will readily see this change as a token of better integration, because the dream's transference context is familiar to them. The same applies if a patient suddenly begins to dream of having had a good relationship with his parents, having hitherto had nothing but very bad images of his relationship with them. Again, if a patient dreams for the first time that his parents are having sexual intercourse, something for which he never previously had a representation, this too appears as a sign of change.

Various kinds of dreams can of course be seen as indicating progress. However, I wish to emphasize that the dreams that turn over a page which I describe in this book have impressed me more than others, because their paradoxical character carries the risk that analyst and patient will fail to understand them as a sign of better integration. This aspect is crucial in terms of psychoanalytic technique.

The fruit of experience

This volume gathers together the results of clinical observation of some of my psychoanalytic patients (analysed on the couch at four sessions a week), as well as the fruits of my reflections, literature searches and many exchanges with colleagues. Coupled with my experience as a supervising psychoanalyst, these gleanings have enabled me to put forward a number of hypotheses on the formation of dreams of this kind.

In a short preliminary paper I described my first observations in terms of their clinical characteristics, without investigating their origin or referring to the psychoanalytic literature on dreams (J.-M. Quinodoz 1987). I showed in particular that these dreams provided us with a wealth of information about hitherto unconscious fantasy contents, and noted that, notwithstanding their primitive character, they arose during phases of integration: 'They appear at key points in the psychoanalytic process – that is, during a phase when the patient is moving on from a regressive to a more mature level of functioning' (1987: 837).

In the ensuing years, further clinical observations accruing from work with my own patients and in supervisions confirmed to me that such dreams occupied a central position in the psychoanalytic process. From the technical standpoint, for example, I realized that, because psychoanalysts were often impressed by the primitive content of these dreams, they were tempted to interpret it even if this intensified the dreamer's anxiety, instead of seeing it in the context of a tendency towards psychic integration. I also came to the conclusion that classical dream theory, which is essentially based on repression, did not adequately account for their formation, and that it was necessary to invoke post-Freudian and contemporary conceptions, such as the notions of unconscious fantasy, oscillation between the paranoid-schizoid and depressive positions, and integration.

I then assembled these observations into a more comprehensive paper (J.-M. Quinodoz 1999), postulating that the paradoxical character of such dreams presumably resulted from a coming together of split-off parts returning to the dreamer's self; this would explain why their primitive content arose during phases of transference integration. I also noted that, whereas similar dreams had been described in the psychoanalytic literature, this particular type differed from them in a number of respects, and it was therefore appropriate to single out dreams that turn over a page and assign them a specific place.

That paper was subsequently presented in an *International Journal of Psycho-Analysis* Internet discussion group, a review of which was published by Paul Williams (1999). Following this stimulating exchange, I felt it appropriate to spell out a number of points in greater detail in this book. For example, the comments received showed me that many psychoanalysts today still interpret dreams predominantly in accordance with classical theory. For this reason, I here briefly recapitulate the broad outlines of the classical theory of dreams, so as to illustrate the nature of the subsequent, post-Freudian, contributions and thereby to bring out their differences and complementarities. I hope that this will provide a better understanding of the foundation on which I have constructed my hypotheses. In addition, I have endeavoured to give a more thorough

7

clinical and theoretical description of the transformations that take place in the transference, facilitating the integration processes which pave the way for the emergence of dreams that turn over a page. I have illustrated these various aspects by a number of clinical examples, one of which – the case of Tania – is presented in detail in Chapter 7. Finally, in view of the unusual clarity and coherence with which such dreams retrospectively illuminate unconscious fantasies, I have examined the parallels observable between the clinical impact of certain dreams and the aesthetic impact of works of art. My reflections here have been particularly stimulated by Hanna Segal's original psychoanalytic publications on dreams and symbolism in relation to art.

Finally, looking back over my hypotheses on dreams that turn over a page, in which I have laid particular stress on integration processes, I noticed that they represent a continuation of the ideas I developed in *The Taming of Solitude* (J.-M. Quinodoz 1991), which dealt with the working through of separation and object-loss anxieties during the psychoanalytic process.

The sense of a metaphor

I coined the phrase 'dreams that turn over a page' spontaneously and for the purposes of personal reference, applying it whenever I came across their identifying characteristics in the fantasy material brought by my analysands or in supervisions, in order to distinguish them from other dreams. Like most of the metaphors we use in psychoanalysis, this one only partially reflects the aspects to which I wish to draw attention. Even so, the use of metaphors for complex psychoanalytic concepts facilitates representation and communication, particularly among psychoanalysts, and my chosen image seems to me more evocative than a technical appellation such as 'dreams with regressive content that appear during a phase of integration'.

The expression 'turning over a page' to my mind suggests a patient's capacity for retrospective representation of a highly significant fantasy arising after the underlying pathology has been overcome. Once this step has been taken, a dream produced in this way in effect enables us to read a message on a page that provides us with the key to solving a puzzle, and, having read it, we feel that we can then turn over the page in order to proceed further. As D. Quinodoz (1994b) points out in relation to the successive processes of remodelling undergone by the self during psychoanalytic treatment, it is not unusual for the last sentence of a chapter or entire novel to alter the meaning of everything that has gone before.

2

A source of uncanny feelings
and anxiety

Anxiety, manifest content and latent content

I have frequently observed that the patient's first reaction on bringing me a dream of this kind is intense anxiety, which he expresses in various ways – for instance: 'I've just had a horrible dream! I'm afraid I shall go mad!' Because these dreams, as it were, put primitive and aggressive fantasies on the stage, the dreamer at first tends to attribute his terror to the manifest dream content, and sometimes the anxiety even causes him momentarily to confuse reality and fantasy. For example, when the female claustrophobic patient mentioned in the previous chapter had a dream of being locked up in prison for life, she initially took its manifest content literally, as if it were concrete reality.

Beyond the manifest content of the dream, the dreamer is also impressed by its latent content – that is, by the multiplicity of unconscious meanings condensed in it and presented in the crude state. Only gradually, in the light of the associations that subsequently bring out their polysemy, will the process of working through with the psychoanalyst allow the dreamer to undo the condensation of these representations and to become conscious of the meaning of the dream's 'text' and its transference dimension.

Hope and anxiety

With regard to the manifest content, in my experience patients often express the fear that their dream might be a sign of retreat just when their intuition tells them that they have made significant progress in their psychic development. This concern may be put into words in different ways: 'Is that where I still am, if I have such a frightening dream? It surely proves that I have not changed!'; 'What

9

use have all those years of psychoanalysis been if all that happens is that I dream of such horrors?'; 'Fancy having a dream like that! It can only mean that I shall never terminate and that I shall need you for the rest of my life!'

By expressing their astonishment in these terms, patients tellingly convey the contradictory feelings aroused by such dreams in the dreamer. However, the patient does so intuitively, without really being conscious of the underlying issues. This ambivalence-laden perplexity then gives rise to a need for the psychoanalyst's help, which in turn constitutes a starting point for the working through of the transference meaning of the dream.

Dream or nightmare?

The anxiety aroused by such dreams raises the question of whether they consistently interrupt the dreamer's sleep and, if so, whether they are akin to nightmares. At first sight, if only the manifest anxiety reaction is considered, these dreams might appear to be nightmares, especially when the dreamer reports that he has been woken up by their frightening content. However, on closer examination, I found that dreams that turn over a page did not systematically awaken the dreamer. In most cases, on waking the dreamer remembers an anxious, uncanny feeling, indicating that the dream did not necessarily interrupt his sleep in the manner characteristic of a nightmare.

Again, in my experience the dreamer's reaction to interpretation differs as between nightmares and dreams that turn over a page. In the former case, the patient's anxiety takes time to wear off and generally remains permanently attached to the content notwithstanding appropriate interpretations. Conversely, *with the type of dream I describe, a judicious interpretation tends to dissipate anxiety quickly*: on the one hand, I have found that an interpretation directed first to the *form* assumed by the dream in the analysand–analyst relationship, and only later to the *content*, is more effective in dissipating anxiety; while, on the other hand, if the dream content includes psychic material pressing to be worked through, the patient will have a different attitude, involving greater receptivity towards the analyst than with evacuative dreams or nightmares. In my view, this difference has to do with the fact that *a dream that turns over a page is one that succeeds – at least partially – in its function of working through, whereas a nightmare fails in this respect*, and therefore has to interrupt the dreamer's sleep.

Uncanny (*unheimlich*) affects and affects of anxiety

So far I have concentrated on the affects of anxiety or fright mentioned by patients initially. However, in my experience, what patients describe as anxiety sometimes appears to me to correspond more to the uncanny (*unheimlich*) affect described by Freud (1919h), which suggests both the familiar (*heimlich*) and the unfamiliar (*un-heimlich*) – that is, the strange or the alien.

Dreamers often express mixed feelings: 'I had a frightening dream last night,' a woman patient told me, 'but oddly enough it did not awaken me.' 'Afterwards, this dream left me with a disturbing impression, something unknown and known at the same time . . .' French-speaking dreamers may even use various forms of the word *inquiétant* [uncanny]: 'I had a dream that troubled [*inquiétée*] me,' another female patient told me, 'it wasn't really anxiety, but the dream left me with a weird feeling.' The translators of the recent French edition of Freud's collected works have chosen the word *inquiétant* because it 'belongs to the same semantic field as *angoissant* [anxiety-inducing] and *effrayant* [frightening], and reproduces the privative prefix *un-* of *unheimlich*' (Bourguignon, Cotet, Laplanche & Robert 1989: 109).[1] However, neither the new French term nor the former translation (*l'inquiétante étrangeté*) has the same force and resonance as *unheimlich* in German.

The uncanny: The 'return' of the repressed and the 'return' of the split-off?

The notion of the uncanny has another dimension too, implying the return of something secret: 'everything is *unheimlich* that ought to have remained secret [*Geheimnis*] and hidden but has come to light' (Freud 1919h: 225). Freud attributes this feeling to various factors, adducing a 'doubling, dividing and interchanging of the self' (ibid.: 234), but the uncanny in his view nevertheless has to do with the mechanism of repression: '[. . .] the frightening element can be shown to be something repressed which *recurs*' (ibid.: 241). In this recurrence, or 'return', Freud stresses only the element of repression; this corresponds to the state of his discoveries in 1919, when he had not yet distinguished the concept of splitting from that of repression. What happens if we introduce this distinction? Might we find that the uncanny feeling reflects the dreamer's reaction to the 'return' not only of repressed contents but, equally, of ones that have been disavowed, split off and projected?

I have placed the word 'return' in quotation marks to indicate that I am using it here in a different sense from what we usually mean by the 'return of the repressed'. As defined by Freud in 1915, the return of the repressed is a process whereby the repressed elements, which do not disappear completely by virtue of repression, tend to reappear, which they do in the distorted form of a compromise (Laplanche & Pontalis 1967: 398). Conversely, what I mean here by 'return' is that psychic contents previously ejected from the ego – whether by repression, disavowal, splitting or projection – are reintegrated into and reappropriated by the ego. Although Freud used the term 'return' mainly in the

1   [Translator's note: The same applies to the English *uncanny*.]

first sense, it certainly also appears in his works in the second, for instance in relation to psychosis:

> There [in neurosis] we see that a reaction of anxiety sets in whenever the repressed instinct makes a thrust forward, and that the outcome of the conflict is only a compromise and does not provide complete satisfaction. Probably in a psychosis the rejected piece of reality constantly forces itself upon the mind, just as the repressed instinct does in a neurosis, and that is why in both cases the consequences too are the same.
>
> (Freud 1924e: 186)

In view of the foregoing, it is my belief that phenomena involving the 'return' of the repressed and of the disavowed are superimposed in the formation of dreams that turn over a page.

The return of projected parts and the consequent threat to the cohesion of the ego

As a dream of this kind may occur during a phase of integration, I have postulated (see Chapter 10) that the ego is confronted with the return of unwanted projections that have not only undergone repression but have also been disavowed, split off and expelled by projective identification into internal or external objects (J.-M. Quinodoz 1999). This 'return' is in my view made possible by various factors connected with the development of the transference relationship, in particular following the working through of the depressive position when the patient arrives at a greater degree of integration. This situation involves a withdrawal of projections and a reinforcement of introjective phenomena, with the result that the split-off parts of the ego can then be accepted as forming part of the self. In other words, *the primitive content of dreams accompanying phases of integration may be said to reflect the 'return' of split-off parts to the ego.* This gives rise to an uncanny feeling when the dreamer is confronted with the resurgence of parts of himself that are both known and unknown, but which nevertheless belong to him. However, it seems to me that the main generator of anxiety is not so much the repressed contents as the perception of splitting phenomena, because these present a threat to the cohesion of the ego itself, as we shall see later.

Another factor to be considered is the fright experienced by the psychotic or the non-psychotic part of the personality when faced with the dawning consciousness of what is unconscious. According to Bion (1992), this is one reason why neurotics fear that a successful psychoanalysis might drive them mad. Bion says that they are then afraid that what is thereby made conscious will never again be able to become unconscious again, and will be for ever lost to unconscious waking thought – a phenomenon perceived by the patient as equivalent to succumbing to psychosis. This suggests that a dreamer confronted with a dream content that has become conscious might fear that it will never be able to return to the unconscious state – something that may partly account for the fear of going mad often expressed in response to such a dream.

The affect of helplessness and the presence of the psychoanalyst

The anxiety triggered by a dream that turns over a page cannot be explained solely by Freud's third theory of anxiety (1940a [1938]), in which splitting plays a major part. We may also invoke his second theory of anxiety, which he here connects with the sense of helplessness (*Hilflosigkeit*) that follows the threat of separation and object loss presented to the ego by danger (Freud 1926d [1925]). From this point of view, we may postulate that the anxiety and feeling of helplessness aroused by such a dream might be one of the determinants of the wish to turn to the psychoanalyst for help: 'I hope that you at least will be able to make something of it!'; 'Tell me what you think of my dream . . . I myself cannot make head or tail of it!'

The need for the psychoanalyst's help, which is expressed by patients in different forms, results from a number of factors; there is a close relationship between patients' capacity to work through a dream and their capacity to recognize the psychoanalyst as a separate and different person, as well as to overcome their ambivalent affects. As we shall see later in relation to similar kinds of dreams, the 'overwhelming dreams' described by Stewart (1992) occur at specific points in the transference relationship – in particular, when patients perceive the presence of the psychoanalyst and tell him that they need his help. Other authors – for instance, Segal (1991) and Grinberg (1967) – have emphasized the part played by the perception of the analyst as a separate, different person in the patient's recognizing that he needs the analyst's support. Bion (1992) not only demonstrates the importance of the analyst's presence when the patient's dream-work-α is defective, but also offers a conception of patient–analyst exchanges that affords a broader approach to the working through of dreams during the psychoanalytic process.

3

Countertransference and containing capacity

For the psychoanalyst

Risk of yielding to the dreamer's anxiety

When a patient brings a dream with primitive content of the type described in my examples, the psychoanalyst may be just as impressed as the dreamer. This is a reaction I have often had myself, and I have also observed it in colleagues during supervisions or clinical presentations. *If it does not occur to the analyst that the patient's anxiety may be an accompaniment to a step in integration, he may be tempted to offer only a partial interpretation of the dream's meaning, thereby risking a reinforcement of the anxiety, instead of interpreting it in the wider context of a stage in the patient's psychic development. Conversely, if the psychoanalyst is able to contain the anxiety and – assuming a sufficient foundation for doing so – to place the dream in the broader context of a stage in the patient's psychic and transference development, the patient's capacity to identify with the analyst's containing function may thereby be strengthened.* That is why it is essential for the analyst to evaluate the overall situation in which the dream arises and to take account of the degree of integration achieved by the patient – an assessment for which every analyst will have his own individual criteria.

Let us consider the example of dreams featuring the death or murder of the analyst, which sometimes occur during the termination period and which express the analysand's hostility towards his analyst. Some psychoanalysts regard these dreams as a manifestation of an end-of-treatment regression and interpret them as a sign that the analysand has not yet achieved an adequate level of integration. Other analysts interpret them differently, as an indication that the patient has become capable of containing, and representing to himself, hitherto intolerable libidinal and aggressive fantasies, considering that these dreams occur at the time of termination. The analyst's view of such dreams and his manner of

14

interpreting them may therefore have differing consequences for the analysand: if the analyst thinks that such a dream is evoking primitive fantasies that have in his opinion been insufficiently worked through, he will tend to prolong the patient's analysis, whereas if he deems the patient to have become capable of tolerating hitherto unrepresentable aspects of himself – in the sense of a dream that turns over a page – he will be more likely to believe that his patient is close to termination.

Projective counteridentification

Besides the risk of yielding to the anxiety connected with the manifest or latent primitive dream content, the analyst faces that of unconsciously giving way to anxieties which the dreamer succeeds in communicating to him by projective identification. In this case the analyst responds by unwittingly succumbing to a projective counteridentification as defined by Grinberg (1962). This is a particular aspect of the analyst's countertransference reaction involving an unconscious identification with a part of the patient's ego that the patient has deposited in him through excessive projective identification.

Two stages can be distinguished in the process of projective counteridentification. The first, which persists until the analyst becomes aware that part of his ego has become confused, without his knowledge, with the part of the ego projected on to him by the analysand, may be seen as a passive attitude on the part of the psychoanalyst, who thus 'succumbs' to his patient's projections. At a second stage, if and when 'the analyst is able to overcome this reaction, he may take advantage of this phenomenon so as to clarify some of the patient's unconscious fantasies and emotions making an adequate interpretation possible' (Grinberg 1979: 237).

The concept of projective counteridentification seems to me to be particularly valuable in connection with dreams that turn over a page in so far as the analyst may initially be tempted to 'yield' passively to the anxious or uncanny affects brought on by them, which the patient may unconsciously deposit in him by pathological projective identification, causing him to experience them as if they were his own. The analyst is then seriously at risk of seeing nothing in the dream but the patient's sadistic drives and destructive fantasies, because he has unwittingly entered into collusion with the patient and is therefore unable either to identify these fantasies or to bind them, in transference interpretations, to the libidinal and reparative drives. However, if the analyst succeeds in consciously distinguishing his own anxiety from that stemming from his patient and in overcoming his reaction, he will be able to adopt an active stance and to interpret the way the patient uses the dream in order to act on the psychoanalyst, with the unconscious aim of avoiding confrontation with the anxieties bound up with better psychic integration.

Capacity to identify with the containing object

Among the transformations that play a major part in the patient's increased capacity to tolerate anxiety, and in particular the anxiety triggered by the occurrence of a dream that turns over a page, the notion of the patient's identification with the analyst's containing capacity seems to me to be one of the most crucial. For it is the working through of the transference relationship that gradually enables the analysand to achieve a better integration of his psychic life during the course of a long and complex developmental process, the main aspects of which will be discussed in the next chapter.

The prospects opened up by Bion (1962) in this field are particularly illuminating with regard to the fate of anxieties and the discovery of the transference/countertransference meaning of dreams that turn over a page. For Bion, the formation of dreams and their interpretations can be understood in the context of a container–contained relationship whereby the analyst uses his 'capacity for reverie' to receive the patient's projections – in particular, dream projections – with a view to returning them to the patient after transforming them and making them tolerable, thus conferring meaning on them. This transformation of β-elements into α-elements applies equally to the different but complementary processes of repression and splitting. In this way, instead of playing a merely passive role, the psychoanalyst who receives the patient's projections becomes an 'active container' (cf. D. Quinodoz 1992).

As I showed in connection with the working through of separation and object-loss anxieties in the psychoanalytic process (J.-M. Quinodoz 1991), the concepts of the container–contained and the 'capacity for reverie' afford a better understanding of the role of normal projective identification as the basis of ego integration. It is after all essential for the conditions for better toleration of pain and anxiety to become established in the patient's mind: if the analysand is to succeed in tolerating anxiety, he must have had the experience of a psychoanalyst capable of understanding and containing him. In this way, the analysand will progressively become capable not only of re-owning the emotional content that has been rendered bearable – that is, the anxiety bound up with the dream contents – but also of introjecting the 'container' – that is, the 'capacity for reverie' of a psychoanalyst capable of tolerating anxiety – and of identifying with such an analyst.

A clinical example: Albert's dream

I've had a crazy dream!

I should now like to present a clinical sequence from an analysis, with a view to illustrating the dreamer's various reactions to a dream that turns over a page, as well as my countertransference reactions and my interpretations within this exchange. To limit the scope of my account, I shall refrain from giving a comprehensive description here of the changes in the transference situation that preceded the occurrence of this dream, as well as those that followed it, as these aspects would call for more thorough development, which I shall provide in the context of a more detailed clinical example – that of Tania – in Chapter 7.

Albert, a patient who had been in psychoanalysis at four sessions a week for several years, one day brought me a dream that surprised me because it included some homosexual fantasy content that had hitherto remained inaccessible to his conscious mind owing to powerful resistances. Having overcome substantial inhibitions and reinforced his heterosexual tendencies, he found this dream all the more disturbing. These advances had been reflected in changes in the transference relationship, while his relations with other people – especially women – in external reality had also improved. On the day in question, he arrived for his session in an unusual state of anxiety. Still distraught, he began: 'I've had a crazy dream which I cannot make head or tail of! In it, I went back to the old house where I used to live with my parents. As I went in, I saw a picture of myself dressed as a girl and a letter addressed to me containing some recipes. I was terrified that I might be taken for a woman and ran away. I found myself sitting on the back seat of a car driven by a couple at a crazier and crazier speed. Suddenly the couple disappeared. I heard a terrible commotion behind me, turned round, and saw a huge lorry driven by a man with a sly look on his face, which crashed into my car from behind; I felt myself being shattered to pieces . . . and that woke me up.' After telling me the dream, and still frightened by it, he exclaimed: 'Am I turning into a homosexual?' Preoccupied by the dream's manifest content, he added: 'I don't get it at all: just when I meet the woman of my life, I dream that I am dressed as a girl and that I am about to get myself raped by a homosexual!'

The associations that followed the dream pointed in several directions. Some confirmed the enrichment he had experienced as a result of the strengthening of his heterosexual inclinations, which had been reflected in a reduction in his aggressive impulses towards myself and a reinforcement of his curiosity about me – as the representative of his parental couple. Moreover, he had succeeded in overcoming his unconscious passive tendencies and in adopting a more active and virile attitude. Referring to his new girlfriend, he told me: 'This time it really is a personal choice that has slowly matured inside me.' Other associations, however, brought back distressing memories of childhood – in particular, the disturbing, sly look on the face of an effeminate teacher.

Countertransference dilemma

Listening to Albert's account of his dream, I had been as surprised as he was that these sadistic homosexual fantasies – of whose transference nature he was aware – had come up just when he had taken some decisive steps in working through the positive aspects of his Oedipus complex. However, while pondering over his associations, I noticed that Albert was becoming more and more anxious.

Some questions came into my mind. Was his fear due solely to the irruption of homosexual fantasies that had been insufficiently worked through and his fear of flying apart mentally, as if calling into question the working through that had been accomplished? Alternatively, in the current phase of his analysis, could I detect, in the dream content and in his associations, grounds for believing that this dream, notwithstanding its primitive content and the violence of its sadism, was an accompaniment to a significant change in his psychic life, so that it could be interpreted as a dream in the process of 'turning over a page'? A number of factors, such as the existence of heterosexual alongside homosexual tendencies, argued in favour of the latter possibility. These heterosexual trends featured, for example, in the wish to rediscover his parental couple and to reinstate them in their function, or in the simultaneous representation of his female and male sides – a sign of better integration of his psychic bisexuality. Finally, this dream seemed to me to reflect Albert's new-found capacity for conscious representation not only of his unconscious passive homosexual fantasies but also of his hitherto disavowed sadistic transference drives.

First stage of interpretation

On the basis of the thoughts that had passed through my mind in quick succession, I decided on a two-stage interpretation. In the first stage, I began by linking the regressive, anxiety-inducing aspects of the dream to Albert's increased capacity for representation and working through, and said: 'If you have been able to dream of being taken for a woman and of being penetrated from behind while fearing that you might be shattered to pieces, might this not be precisely because you have become capable of tolerating aspects of yourself that arouse anxiety – aspects that you never dared to imagine before – and of dreaming about them?' I added: 'And in this dream, are you not also showing how angry you are with me for making you realize how much you envy your mother, whose place with your father – represented by me – you would like to take? But at the same time, are you not also showing how much you appreciate knowing me better – as a man, father and husband of your mother – so that you can assert yourself better as a man?' Albert seemed to accept all this with perfect good humour and immediately regained his composure, as if nothing disturbing had happened, and he seemed to have no inkling that my interpretation had modified some unconscious primitive defences. What had in fact been the function of this first interpretation? I believe that it had had effects on different levels. For instance, by showing Albert that he was more capable of the representation of unrecognized aspects of himself – such as homosexual wishes or long-suppressed violent aggressive feelings towards me – I was enabling him to identify with me in my capacity to contain his own anxieties. Moreover, in my interpretations I was putting together different partial aspects of his experience, thereby reinforcing his capacity to recover the fragments of his ego that had been scattered by splitting and projective identification.

I was thereby paving the way for the second stage of the interpretation, by seeking to strengthen the dreamer's ego and to give it enough cohesion and integration for dream work and the capacity to symbolize to be exercised within a unified ego capable of due repression. After all, if the dream work as defined in classical theory is to be able to operate fully on the manifest and latent contents, the dreamer's ego must have achieved a sufficient degree of cohesion and integration, and that is the clinical material to which the second-stage interpretations are directed. In Albert's case, however, I shall not discuss the second stage of the analysis of this dream that turned over a page, as a detailed description of the complexity of the changes accomplished would take us too far.

4

Progress and retreat in response to progress

Reversal of the classical sequence

In examining dreams that turn over a page, we find that they arise *after* and not *before* a significant change, so that the expected classical sequence is here reversed. As a rule, after all, the patient is supposed first to become conscious of resistances and work them through, and only then to resolve conflicts in consequence: 'our work is aimed directly at finding out and overcoming the "resistances", and we can justifiably rely on the complexes coming to light without difficulty as soon as the resistances have been recognized and removed' (Freud 1910d: 144). Whereas this sequence is observed in patients with a neurotic structure, we do not encounter it in all patients – especially those in whom primitive defences predominate.

Commenting on the reversal of the classical sequence in these dreams, which I described in 1999, Ponsi (quoted by Williams 1999) noted that, if only the classical scheme of reference is applied, dreams that turn over a page do indeed not conform to the usual mechanism of dream formation and interpretation. However, if such dreams are considered in a contemporary-style relational context, their paradoxical character is less obvious, because the emphasis in this case is, in Ponsi's view, not so much on the content of the dream as an intrapsychic product, in accordance with the classical approach, as on the narration of the dream as it unfolds in the psychoanalytic situation. It does seem to me that, to account for the occurrence of such a dream, we must not only adopt the classical approach to dream formation but also invoke a contemporary conception that involves the vicissitudes of the transference–countertransference relationship, as well as the concept of psychic integration, in its production.

Dream formation in the context of the transference

The idea that the transference and dream production are closely connected is by no means new, as Freud himself saw transference interpretation as the foundation of psychoanalytic activity and connected the analysis of dreams with it. However, the classical approach did not assign such a central position to the direct and continuous interpretation of the patient–analyst relationship as most psychoanalysts do today. Again, in classical Freudian theory, the content of dreams was understood primarily as the expression of repressed drive wishes, which were interpreted by analysis of resistances and defences – the context being more that of reconstructing the infantile past than of systematic transference analysis. Even if dream interpretation has not always been so closely linked to the vicissitudes of the transference, it has nevertheless been deemed a major dimension of technique since the beginnings of psychoanalysis. Indeed, in the 1930s the technique of dream interpretation was considered to be virtually equivalent to psychoanalytic technique proper (Sharpe 1937).

From the 1950s on, the formation of dreams came increasingly to be seen in a broader relational context – more so than it had been in Freud's conception. This is emphasized by Flanders in her well-documented editorial introduction to *The Dream Discourse Today*, which presents a cross-section of the main psychoanalytic contributions on dream analysis over the last three decades: 'the focus of a contemporary analysis is emphatically the dreamer, not the dream. The aim of an analysis is to facilitate emotional growth through understanding derived principally from the interplay of the transference and counter-transference' (Flanders 1993: 20). Hence, according to today's prevailing view, dream formation primarily reflects the patient–analyst relationship as experienced during the psychoanalytic process, so that the transference relationship is essentially understood and interpreted in the light of the dream contents that reflect it. Although dream analysis seems to have been partially ousted from the central position it occupied in the past, Flanders points out that most contemporary psychoanalytic contributions still include clinical material incorporating the analysis of at least one dream, because it is through dreams that patients talk about themselves best.

Integration and working through of separation anxieties

The progressive work of integration whereby dreams assume meaning during the development of the analysand–analyst relationship depends on a large number of factors, among which the working through of separation and object-loss anxieties plays an important part (J.-M. Quinodoz 1991). After all, patients in psychoanalysis are constantly confronted with the need to work through and mourn fantasized or actual losses and separations from the psychoanalyst, in particular in relation to the end of sessions, weekends and holidays. The reactivation of psychic pain in the transference results in a concomitant re-inforcement of the conflict of ambivalence; and the conscious and unconscious resurgence of hate for the analyst – representing at one and the same time the loved and the hated object – puts the psychoanalyst's countertransference sorely to the test. 'Yet it is the analyst's capacity to accept these projections in the transference that will allow him to distinguish aggression from destructiveness and to link it with positive feelings, in order to restore the connection between love and hate' (ibid.: 131).

These transformations in the transference affects have repercussions not only on the patient's object relations but also on his ego structure, as well as on his capacity to work through his dreams and grasp their symbolic meaning. Again, when introjective processes take over from those of projection and projective identification, we find that the patient is better able to tolerate anxiety, separation and object loss, as well as the feeling of solitude. In my experience, the capacity to tolerate solitude in phases of integration reflects an increased sense of the individual's cohesion and unity, connected with the gathering together of the scattered parts of the ego, which I have described as 'buoyancy' (J.-M. Quinodoz 1991).

Criteria for evaluating progress and integration

When we are confronted with a dream exhibiting primitive content that we would like to place in a broader context to help us decide whether it indicates retreat and insufficient integration or, conversely, belongs to a phase of progress, what criteria should we use as the basis of our evaluation? A number of criteria have been put forward for the psychoanalytic assessment of patients' increased integration capacity. These include not only external criteria, such as the disappearance of symptoms or anxiety or the lifting of inhibitions, but also internal ones connected with the development of the transference relationship and its repercussions on the patient's psychic structure.

Whereas external marks of change are easier to evaluate because they are more readily identifiable, internal criteria of changes in the processes of psychic integration – extending beyond classical ones such as the transition from the primary to the secondary process – are more complex and more difficult to pinpoint. This is because the evaluation of psychic transformations depends also, and to a substantial extent, on the individual psychoanalytic conceptions applied by each analyst to take account of his observations, as well as on his own experience.

I personally use the following criteria of better psychic functioning: the diminution of projective mechanisms (in particular, projective identification) in favour of introjection; sufficient capacity to move on from the paranoid-schizoid position to the depressive position (entailing a reduction in primitive defences such as disavowal, splitting, omnipotence and projection); and the perception of the analyst as a separate, different person. Other criteria are the predominance of love over hate, and an increased capacity on the part of the patient to tolerate depressive affects, sadness, guilt and the sense of solitude.

Progress and retreat in response to progress and regression

From a developmental point of view, dreams that turn over a page may be regarded psychoanalytically as falling within a context of simultaneous progress and regression. The notion of progress and regression is after all implicit in that of development, and in these terms the psychosexual maturation of a child can be described as a succession of stages each representing a step forward in learning. However, each step forward may be accompanied by momentary phases of regression, which do not necessarily imply that the child is taking a step back in its development. Mahler *et al.* (1975) refer to these phases as necessary moments when the child recharges its batteries or undertakes 'refuelling'. Similarly, René Diatkine has drawn attention to the importance of parents accepting that a child or adolescent may experience temporary episodes of regression as a 'replenishment of his well-springs' and not being alarmed by them.

In my description so far of the characteristics of dreams that turn over a page, I have used the terms 'progress' and 'regression' to take account of the fact that such dreams occur just when the patient is taking a step in psychic development – which may be regarded as progress – whereas their archaic, aggressive content could be seen as a token of regression. On reflection, it seems to me that the concepts of progress and regression do not always adequately describe the phenomena we observe, having regard to their transference dimension. For these notions may come to constitute value judgements and give rise to mis-understanding, if progress is seen solely in positive terms and regression negatively – considering that regression is crucial in any attempt to reach and work through the contents of the deepest layers of the mind. In such a case, interpretations would have the undesirable consequence of creating a split between an idealization of progress and a denigration of regression – the very antithesis of one of the aims of psychoanalysis, which is to increase the dreamer's capacity to contain the various aspects of psychic experience so that they can be contemplated as a whole. To avoid misunderstandings, I have therefore sought to introduce a differentiation in my use of the terms 'progress' and 'regression', by placing these transference phenomena in a context of incessant oscillations between phases of progress and phases of retreat in response to progress, or between phases of integration and phases of retreat in response to integration.

Recurrence of ambivalence

The uncanny and anxious feelings of a dreamer confronted with the archaic content of a dream that turns over a page, as well as with aggression and destructiveness, usually have the effect of reinforcing ambivalence towards the psychoanalyst. It is therefore important for the psychoanalyst to identify such anxieties in order to provide the optimum conditions for integration of affects by the patient. *For the dreamer's capacity to overcome transference ambivalence proves to be intimately connected with his capacity to work through a dream. If he succeeds in becoming conscious of the hostility towards the analyst revealed by such a dream, he will be better able to grasp its symbolic meaning and accept interpretations. Conversely, the persistence of failure to recognize a transference ambivalence is likely to prevent the dream from performing its function of working through, so that it does not truly succeed in 'turning over a page'.*

For example, if the primitive fantasies and sadism of the dream contents impress the dreamer, as we have seen, he will surely be even more impressed on becoming conscious of the aggression that such a dream may unleash towards the psychoanalyst. The more difficult he finds it to link these component affects consciously to the positive transference affects and fantasies of reparation that may also be identified in the dream content, the more dangerous and destructive will be his experience of them. For instance, when a patient exclaims: 'I've had a frightening dream; is that as far as I've got in my analysis if I still have such dreams?', is he not thereby indirectly blaming the analyst for not protecting him sufficiently from his own aggression and destructive anxieties? And when, after dreaming of a lorry driver who crashed his vehicle into the back of his car, Albert declared: 'Am I becoming a homosexual?', was it not me – his psychoanalyst – whom he was accusing of driving myself towards him like a dangerous homosexual seducer?

If the psychoanalyst intends to help the dreamer to begin to overcome ambivalence, it is therefore essential for him to identify both the hostile and the positive feelings the patient is projecting on to his person, so that the patient can become conscious of them. The analyst will then be able to offer interpretations that will promote links between the libidinal and aggressive currents of the transference, as well as between idealization and denigration of the object, with a view to integrating them better within a whole-object relationship as the depressive position is worked through.

Returning to the case of Albert, we find that, alongside hostile transference sentiments, various positive feelings were discernible in the dream content and associations. For instance, his heterosexual desires were represented through his wish to rediscover his parents' bedroom, with the aim of identifying with his father and his parental couple, or of imagining his male and female parts within the framework of a more assimilated psychic bisexuality. At transference level, Albert had expressed his gratitude to me for his changed attitude to women, and not merely the resentment due to this dream. In my interpretations I was thus able not only to draw attention to his new capacity for representing hitherto unrepresentable aspects of himself in a dream, but also to point out that, having come to see me more as a whole person, he could now accept hating and appreciating me at one and the same time.

In other words, the patient's capacity to become conscious of, and to overcome, his ambivalent transference affects helps to provide him with the psychic resources for using his dream and gaining access to its symbolic meaning.

Ambivalence and the negative therapeutic reaction

The fact that the primitive content of a dream that turns over a page may be experienced by the dreamer as a threat of deterioration in his condition, and that the analyst may see and interpret it in the same way, raises the issue of the relationship between such dreams and a negative therapeutic reaction – for example, when the patient's response to a frightening dream is: 'I thought I was getting better, but after this dream I am afraid of going mad!', or 'Fancy having a dream like that; it can only mean that I shall never finish my analysis!'

Freud drew attention early on (1914g) to the problem of the exacerbation of the conflicts and the recurrence of symptoms in a patient who was getting better, when the patient used resistance in order to remain ill. In this sense, a patient may – unconsciously – try to use the primitive and frightening content of a dream that turns over a page for the purpose of *acting* on the analyst in the session, in order to demonstrate to him that he has not acquired an adequate capacity to contain and work through his anxiety at the progress achieved.

For example, noting the occurrence of dreams corresponding to dreams that turn over a page in two patients, C. Hering (personal communication) drew my attention to the way in which some patients occasionally produce an impressive and clamorous anxiety dream with the unconscious aim of intimidating the psychoanalyst. To all appearances, the patient is doing his best to demonstrate not only to himself but also to his analyst that he is not yet strong enough, and lacks the capacity, to tolerate the anxiety bound up with his progress. In Hering's opinion, such dreams are intended to dissuade the dreamer from pursuing his development, and are similar in some respects to a negative therapeutic reaction. This observation confirms how important it is for the analyst to emphasize the patient's capacity to contain anxiety and, in his interpretations, to link progress with retreat in response to progress.

5

Retrospective illumination

Direct access to the unconscious 'program'?

As noted earlier on the basis of my own observations, dreams that turn over a page surprise the analyst because they *reveal the unconscious fantasies underlying transference conflicts with greater clarity and precision than ordinary dreams. Appearing as they do after a change, they retrospectively illuminate its underlying unconscious structure, bringing to light not only repressed but also disavowed and split-off contents.*

It is as if the psychoanalyst suddenly had access to the 'programs' or 'program sources codes' that are the hidden vehicle of the dreamer's unconscious conflicts – highly significant conflicts whose existence the psychoanalyst could hitherto only surmise and to which he did not have genuine access. Again, such dreams have the advantage of revealing the unconscious fantasy in the patient's 'own individual iconography', as O'Shaughnessy (2000: 32–3) judiciously observed in connection with a similar dream: 'What I had recognised only partially and in general terms, that Mrs A was not fully participant, that strong feelings were given coherent meaning by her dream, which reveals the whole of a deep defensive phantasy'. In other words, dreams of this kind not only throw particular light on past relational contexts and present–day transference-related ones, which have undergone repression or been split off, but also give us information on the organization of the underlying defensive processes. These, as we know, may be experienced, described or represented in dreams and fantasies, as Segal (1964) has shown.

The role of unconscious fantasy

In view of the central role of the concept of unconscious fantasy in my understanding of the dynamics of dreams that turn over a page, it is, I believe, worth recalling here that, although this notion was introduced by Freud, we owe the full development of its implications to Klein (1934, 1940) and Isaacs (1948).

26

Freud's conception of unconscious fantasy differs markedly from the Kleinian and post-Kleinian view. Freud distinguished daydream-like conscious fantasies from unconscious fantasies, the latter in his view being the result of repression of a wish repudiated by the ego, which assumes the form of a compromise that can reappear in the guise of a symptom or dream. In the Freudian conception, fantasies are highly organized phenomena that refer essentially to whole objects and appear relatively late on; for this reason, primitive fantasies feature hardly at all in his description, as Segal (1991) points out. As for the primal fantasies persisting in the unconscious, Freud attributes them to real events handed down from the earliest days of mankind.

Klein (1934, 1940) adds a wider and more important dimension to the notion of unconscious fantasy. In her view, such fantasies are active from the beginning of life, are the direct expression of the drives, and have to do with the relations between self and objects. One of the fundamental differences between the Freudian and Kleinian conceptions is that, in the latter, all fantasy activity stems from the ego, and that there exists from the beginning an ego with sufficient capacity to experience anxiety, to form a kind of object relationship at reality and fantasy level, and to deploy primitive defences. Segal gives an evocative description of the differences between Freud's conception of unconscious fantasy and Klein's:

> Most of Freud's statements give the impression that he thought of unconscious phantasies as if they were like islands in the sea of mental life. Reading Klein's work with children, one gets a glimpse of an internal phantasy world like a vast continent under the sea, the islands being its conscious, external, observable manifestations.
>
> (Segal 1991: 19)

In my view, a wider conception of unconscious fantasy can explain why the psychoanalyst is genuinely surprised by the coherence with which the content of a dream of this kind retrospectively supplies the key to solving the puzzle presented by a prior change, which it has not yet been possible to elucidate on the basis of the available clinical material. It was this aspect that specifically attracted my attention when, in 1987, I noted at the outset the unusual precision with which some dreams exposed the 'primal matrix of fantasy' in all its rich complexity to the observing psychoanalyst.

Unconscious fantasy, drives, defences and personality structure

The Kleinian conception of unconscious fantasy is in my view essential because it helps us to realize that most dreams, and in particular dreams that turn over a page, are not merely the expression of repressed conflicts but also reflect the organization of drives and defences, as well as the structure of the personality.

According to Klein, unconscious fantasies have both a wish-fulfilling and a defensive aspect from the very beginning of life; she considers that not only libidinal and aggressive impulses towards objects, but also defence mechanisms, feed into unconscious fantasies. Moreover, unconscious fantasies are intimately linked to personality structure, as Segal (1991) points out. In Freud's structural model, the internal fantasy objects that create our personality are determined not only by the reality of the object introjected in fantasy, but also by the child's projections on to that object. It is the early fantasies of projection and introjection present from the beginning of life that constitute the foundation of personality structure.

Similarities to 'recapitulative dreams'

The notion of unconscious fantasy seems to me to be implicit in the description given by Guillaumin (1979) of the properties of certain dreams that highlight conflicts and the concomitant search for a resolution. He calls such dreams 'recapitulative' or 'synthetic'. They take the form of a '*sequence of connected episodes*, corresponding to a *dialectical progression in defence*, which follows an ascending genetic order (in the direction of development)'. Another of their characteristics is that they 'offer *great coherence* at a deep level to interpretation, so that they readily appear as focused on *the exposition of the elements* (at successive levels), and on the *negotiation*, of a *conflict* [. . .] that is closely connected, in the context of an analysis, with the subject's *most important and fundamental problems* (the "basic" complex or conflict)'. Guillaumin points out, too, that these dreams tend towards '*the dramatic expression of an active solution*' and closely foreshadow '*actual developments in the subject's psychic behaviour*, especially in the context of the transference' (p. 106, Guillaumin's emphasis). I shall have more to say later about the value of the concept of recapitulative dreams and about other similarities between them and dreams that turn over a page.

Emergence of unconscious homosexual tendencies

I have often observed that the content of the dreams described in this book reveals unconscious fantasies connected with deep-lying homosexual tendencies, which have never before appeared in such sharp focus. For instance, in my two extensive clinical examples – Albert in Chapter 3 and Tania in Chapter 7 – we observe the emergence of latent homosexual fantasies, juxtaposed with others connected with genital psychosexuality. In this way the aspects of the personality that are both masculine and feminine become psychically representable and coexist as symbolic representations, and not only as concrete symbols in which the fact of having and dreaming of homosexual fantasies is experienced more or less as actually being homosexual. Such juxtapositions can be found in the male patient described by Rosenfeld (1987) and in O'Shaughnessy's (2000) female patient; I shall discuss these clinical examples in Chapter 10.

Reflecting on the possible reasons for the frequent emergence of homosexual fantasies in dreams of this kind, I have concluded that they result from a two-fold process combining splitting and repression. On the one hand, these fantasies have remained permanently outside consciousness by virtue of the mechanisms of disavowal and splitting. They resurface with the development of the trans-ference relationship when better psychic integration allows the 'return' to the ego of split-off fragments, which strike the psychoanalyst as enormously significant. On the other hand, *as splitting wanes, the working through of the depressive position leads to better ego–object differentiation, so that repression begins to operate, while symbolic representation replaces primitive forms of symbolism. There then arise elements of representations linked to an increased capacity on the part of the patient to represent his male and female sides simultaneously.* It is these elements that argued in favour of a better integration of psychic bisexuality in Albert, when I detected the presence of indicators not only of 'the man's passive female position' but also of female genital psychosexuality.

It might be objected that the appearance here of such significant dream contents means that they have not been adequately identified, interpreted and worked through. The possibility certainly does occur to one. In my experience, however, this situation results not so much from failure to identify such contents as from the combined effect of resistances and defence mechanisms that make it difficult for the patient to become conscious of them, despite repeated attempts at interpretation by the analyst. As a result, the analyst has a sense of satisfaction when these fantasies eventually do appear in the clinical material, especially if they then bear out his prior working hypotheses.

PART TWO

Interpretations

6

Interpreting in two stages

Why two stages?

When confronted with these anxiety-inducing dreams that arise after decisive changes, I noticed that, if the dream content was interpreted only along classical lines – for example, as the fulfilment of an unsatisfied wish – the dreamer's anxiety tended to persist, sometimes even extending over several sessions. I gradually came to realize the paramount importance of a first stage of interpretation at the point of urgency, where the anxiety is strongest. This means giving interpretations whose aim is to enable the patient to regain his momentarily disturbed capacity for thought and elaboration. At a second stage, once the patient's anxiety has died down, the psychoanalyst will be able to go on to interpret the dream contents proper.

For this purpose, the psychoanalytic work will initially involve placing the dream in the context of the overall transference situation, considered as a whole, without focusing one's interpretations on analysis of the dream content (this will be reserved for the later stage):

> As I suggested, following only the content of the dream has its limitations. If we analyse not the dream but the dreamer, and take into account the form of the dream, the way it is recounted, and the function it performs in the session, our understanding is very much enriched and we can see how the dream's function throws an important light on the functioning of the ego.
>
> (Segal 1991: 73)

First stage of interpretation

Containing the primitive aspects of experience

The aim of this first stage of interpretation is to achieve a preliminary degree of binding and integration of the scattered aspects of the experience of both patient and analyst in response to the emergence of a dream of the kind with which we are here concerned.

For example, when the psychoanalyst succeeds in identifying a link between the appearance of a dream with primitive content and an increased capacity for integration in the patient's experience, he will be able to show the dreamer that his disturbing dream is not necessarily a sign that he is seriously ill or going mad, as he imagines, but may instead reflect his increased capacity for representation of hitherto inaccessible unconscious fantasies.

In most cases such an interpretation will be found to dissipate the anxiety relatively quickly, because it has the effect of reducing splits and encouraging the working through of the depressive position. After all, one of the principal accomplishments of the depressive position is a capacity on the part of the individual for better integration and containment of primitive aspects of his experience.

Again, *this interpretive approach is based on the distinction between different levels of psychic functioning, namely splitting processes and processes of repression. For the patient's ego must have achieved a sufficient degree of cohesion and unity for repression to operate, and for the dreamer to be able to elaborate the symbolic meaning of the dream contents. For this reason, the first stage of interpretation will relate to the patient's capacity to integrate the split-off parts of his ego, so that the subsequent interpretations of content can be given in the context of a unified ego within which the mechanism of repression can replace that of splitting.*

Interpretation with a view to binding

Owing to the importance of splitting and fragmentation phenomena in the formation of dreams, and in particular of dreams that turn over a page, it is essential for the psychoanalyst to identify the scattered fragments of experience so that they can undergo binding. This work will involve, for example, the bringing together of the various split-off parts of the self and of objects, or the binding together of aggressive and libidinal drives. The analyst will find the relevant material in the manifest and latent dream content, in the dreamer's associations, and in his own countertransference experience.

As we have seen in connection with ambivalence, it is therefore important for the interpretations given to bring together the sadism unconsciously expressed by the patient in the transference and the libidinal drives which he is equally unaware of expressing. Similarly, in the case of Albert, it was vitally important for my interpretations to re-establish links between the anxiety generated by the emergence of his latent homosexual tendencies and his new capacity to contain and represent to himself the sadistic fantasies entailed by his relationship with me, as well as his unconscious wish to be, and fear of being, penetrated from behind and of flying apart. When the scattered components have been identified, it will be possible to construct an interpretation that will bind the fear of a retreat in response to the progress that is taking place, along the following lines: 'It seems to me that, if you have been able to bring such disturbing aspects in this dream, it is probably because you have become capable of representing to yourself some hidden tendencies which you were unable to tolerate until now and which we shall now be able to look at together more closely.'

Interpretations both precise and unsaturated

As formulated, the above interpretation constitutes an initial outline expressed in general terms; it needs to be fleshed out and made more specific in accordance with the situation of the transference relationship at the relevant time. In this connection, I should like to make the same point as I did in relation to the interpretation of separation anxieties during psychoanalytic treatment. *If our interpretations are too general and not precise enough, they may quickly descend into reductiveness and repetition. It is therefore essential for the psychoanalyst to take detailed account of the particular moment in the treatment, which is never repeated identically* (J.-M. Quinodoz 1991). On the basis of the foregoing, the interpretation of dreams that turn over a page may then constitute a vital opportunity for interpreting crucial aspects of the analysand–analyst relationship in the heat of the session.

It is in my view also important for us to give 'unsaturated' interpretations that invite the patient to understand himself in an open way, and to listen out for what the patient is telling us, in particular through the 'narrative derivatives of the alpha elements' identified in the fantasy material (Ferro 2000). By thus paying attention to the patient's active contribution, we shall remain constantly in touch with his perception of our interpretations.

Interpreting the dream's function

Another important preliminary to analysis of the dream contents proper is identification of the *function* performed by the dream in the session and of the way the patient acts on the psychoanalyst through the dream, with a view to interpreting it. This approach is based on Segal's distinction between interpretation of the dream's *content* and interpretation of its *function*. She showed that there may be no point in trying to give only a classical interpretation of the content of certain patients' dreams, for instance when the dream work is deficient. It is only after the way the dream is used in the session has been interpreted that analysis of the content can ensue. In her opinion, these dreams are often used for the purpose of acting out in the session, and it is primarily this function that must be interpreted: 'Some patients come flooding the analyst with dreams and confusion. In such a case the first thing to interpret is the flooding and the effect it is supposed to have on the analyst. [. . .] Only gradually, and where it connects with this function, can one address the actual content of the dream' (Segal 1991: 72).

For example, after such a dream the dreamer may not only expel the anxiety-inducing dream contents into the psychoanalyst's mind, but at the same time also expel his own capacity to contain and work through anxiety. Before interpreting the dream contents proper, it is therefore of paramount importance for the psychoanalyst first to show the patient how he is using his dream in the session. In the case of dreams that turn over a page, we have already seen how a patient may unconsciously use the anxiety accompanying a dream to try to make the analyst believe that he (the patient) is incapable of tolerating progress and that this belief is shared by each without the other's knowledge. What must be interpreted is how the patient uses the dream to *act this out*.

Interpretation in projection

The patient's identification with the psychoanalyst's containing function contributes to the relief observable when the various aspects of a dream's transference function are interpreted. This enables the dreamer to re-own the 'healthy' part of himself – the part that is capable of thinking and symbolizing – which he had discarded at the same time as the unwanted dream contents. For these reasons, interpreting the patient's identification with the containing capacity of the psychoanalyst helps draw attention to a constructive aspect of the transference relationship, which may be put together with other – hostile or destructive – aspects.

Sometimes, however, interpretations at verbal and symbolic level have no effect on the anxiety, which the patient is unable to contain, and in this case recourse must be had to a different form of interpretation – namely, interpretation in projection as described by D. Quinodoz (1994a). Such an interpretation in these circumstances often has the effect of relieving the patient's anxiety, as the analyst's direct verbalization of the patient's words gives rise to a mirror effect that allows the patient to calm down: after a moment of confusion, the patient recognizes his own words and can re-own the aspects for which the analyst has made himself the spokesperson. Being suddenly induced to distinguish between what comes from the analyst and what comes from himself, the patient then rediscovers the feelings that are his own, as well as the capacity to contain and work through his anxieties.

Is this a genuine interpretation?

Can an interpretation that links the patient's capacity to represent repudiated aspects of himself in a dream with his identification with the analyst's capacity to contain anxiety genuinely be deemed an interpretation? This objection has sometimes been raised by colleagues who seem essentially to be adopting a classical approach based on the analysis of dream contents. In my view, it takes no account of the value of interpreting in the transference the role played by the containing capacity of the object; nor does it address the function performed by the dream before interpretation of its contents where the dream work is itself deficient. In Segal's opinion, the relative pessimism about dream interpretation that has arisen in the last few years is partly due to attempts to analyse dreams solely in accordance with the classical approach.

The point is that the various levels to which interpretations are addressed must be distinguished. In the classical situation, an interpretation is directed first and foremost to the repressed contents – that is to say, it is aimed at patients with a neurotic organization, which means that they have reached a level on which the symbolic function allows them to grasp the unconscious meaning of conflicts, so that they can verbalize them. However, in the case of a mental apparatus disorganized by disavowal, splitting and projective identification, the psychoanalyst must give interpretations directed towards the effects of the primitive defences on the structure of the ego itself. Only then, at a second stage, once the ego has regained its capacity to integrate, will the psychoanalyst be able to offer interpretations of repressed contents, repression having gradually taken the place of splitting.

Second stage of interpretation

Transition between the two stages

The effect of the first-stage interpretations is as a rule to awaken the dreamer's curiosity about the meaning of the dream contents. *A new phase then ensues in the elaboration of the dream, characterized by the patient's wish to use the psychoanalyst as a separate, different object, with a view to elucidating the manifest and latent meaning of the dream at symbolic level.* To this end, the second stage of interpretation will be based on the patient's increased capacity for symbolic representation and for tolerating detailed analysis of repressed as well as split-off contents, and for this purpose the analyst will apply classical techniques enriched with post-Freudian contributions.

However, in order for the first-stage interpretation to be effective and to allow the patient to recover his capacity to think and symbolize, the ground must first have been prepared for this transition. For there is no magic way of enabling the patient to move on from a form of psychic functioning in which anxiety and primitive defences predominate to a more mature form. This development is conditional upon a number of transformations that gradually promote better communication at both internal and external level. What are the factors that facilitate the transition from a primitive symbolic form of functioning to one based on genuine symbolism or symbolic representation?

Onset of symbolic representation

As we have seen, changes in the function of dreams take place when the patient seeks in the person of the psychoanalyst an object with which to identify in its containing capacity, with a view to recovering his own capacity to think and to work through his dream. This recognition of the need for the analyst's help results from changes that have gradually ensued during the course of the transference process, whereby the analyst comes to be better perceived as a separate, different person with an existence of his own, and with whom the function of symbolic communication can be established at verbal level.

For unconscious fantasy is expressed through symbolism, and true symbolism lies at the root of insight and verbalization, which are characteristic of neurotic functioning. *In order for a patient to realize that the manifest meaning of his words refers back to a latent sense, he must possess an adequate capacity for symbolization. If not, he will be unable to 'detach himself' from the manifest sense, and any interpretation by the analyst of the latent sense will seem to him to be mad.* The full operation of the function of symbolic representation calls, in Segal's view, for a tripartite relationship, and for this purpose a sufficient distinction must be established between 'the symbol, the object it symbolizes, and the person for whom the symbol is the symbol of the object. In the absence of a person there can be no symbol' (Segal 1991: 38). However, this three-term relationship no longer holds good when projective identification increases, as the concordant part of the self is identified with the object, so that the self is insufficiently differentiated from the object itself; the symbol is then confused with what is symbolized. We then have a primitive form of symbolization, the *symbolic equation*, which underlies the psychotic's concrete thought and constitutes the basis of pathological mourning.

The possibility of distinguishing between two kinds of symbol formation and of symbolic function is important because of its relevance to the linkage between the two stages observed in the formation of dreams that turn over a page. In the first stage, as a result of projective identification and excessive anxiety, concrete symbolism tends to predominate. In the second stage, however, if anxiety and projective mechanisms decline and discrimination between self and object increases, true symbolism or symbolic representation may become established, so that the symbol can be perceived as representing the object but not as equivalent to it.

The two modes of symbolization also correlate with different levels of anxiety: the symbolic equation is characteristic of the paranoid-schizoid position, whereas true symbolism or symbolic representation is associated with the depressive position. Note, too, that there are transitional forms between the two extremes, and, furthermore, that the symbolism of the depressive position always coexists with concrete symbolic elements in varying proportions. Again, as Segal points out, symbols already formed and operating as true symbols may return to the state of the symbolic equation, so that the dream content may for example be acted out in the transference relationship during the session, as we shall see later in connection with the female patient described by O'Shaughnessy (2000).

Symbolic reparation

At the onset of the depressive position, with the experience of being separate and alone and the perception of separateness and loss, symbolic representation comes into play and internal symbolic reparation can operate (Segal 1991).

A dream then no longer appears to the dreamer as the equivalent of concrete events in which there is little difference between hallucination, dreaming and reality, and which operates as a symbolic equation or expulsion of β-elements. Instead it becomes a means of intrapsychic communication between the dreamer's conscious and unconscious, as well as a means of communication in the patient–analyst relationship. The dream can then fully perform its function, which is that of a metaphorical expression of unconscious conflicts and a search for a fantasy solution to them; and this expression takes the symbolic representational form of a wish fulfilment.

To sum up, my reason for distinguishing two stages in the interpretation of these dreams is to emphasize that the function of a dream is performed at different levels, which the psychoanalyst must identify in order to interpret on the appropriate one. Even though the unconscious problem situation has been clearly set out through the dream content, its symbolic meaning will be fully assimilated only to the extent that the dreamer has integrated it into the transference/countertransference relationship.

Interpretations of a dream that turns over a page: Tania's dream

Unconscious motivation of a request for analysis

Intense ambivalence

To illustrate how a dream that turns over a page can subsequently throw light on a change and reveal the unconscious fantasies that had previously blocked the development in question, I have chosen to present a sequence from the psychoanalysis of a woman patient whom I shall call Tania, whose treatment ended many years ago. For this purpose, I shall begin with a detailed account of the transference situation during the period preceding this dream, to give the reader an idea of the complex unconscious constellation that was retrospectively to be illuminated by the dream content.

Tania had come to me for analysis after repeated failures in her attempts to form a lasting relationship with men; she had been married once, but the marriage had lasted only a few months. In addition, she was afraid of getting too old to have children. She also had serious inhibitions that stood in the way of her career achievement. In her affective life, she was attracted by men, and to some extent by women too. When Tania 'took a fancy' to a man, as she put it, she did everything possible to seduce him, but once he had been conquered, she soon became contemptuous and rejecting. A break would ensue, leaving her both depressed and angry. However, as soon as she found herself alone again, Tania would bemoan her lot, saying that she simply *had* to have a man in order to blossom as a woman; she therefore could not rest until she found a new partner, but then the whole scenario would be repeated. Her attraction to women manifested itself in the way Tania and her woman friends spent hours complaining together about the disappointing experiences they had had with men, by whom they felt victimized. During her adolescence Tania had had a brief homosexual experience with an older woman, which had aroused intense guilt and reinforced her ambivalence towards not only men but also women.

Professionally, too, Tania had ambivalent feelings and inhibitions that prevented her from achieving her ambitions. Not without difficulty, she had succeeded in passing her final examinations at university, but the responsible position she had obtained when she began work was well below her level of competence. In her job, she felt relatively worthless, mainly because she was a woman and not a man, and because 'power' lay exclusively in the hands of men. However, she gradually became aware that she was not only the victim of men but also of her own low self-esteem. On account of this twofold sense of failure – on the levels of both femininity and career – she thought she would try psychoanalysis 'to do something to get myself out of it'. The treatment lasted more than five years at four sessions a week.

Drawing of battle lines in the initial interviews

When Tania told me her story for the first time, I quickly realized that the transference situation would revolve around her intense ambivalence, for the patient could neither detach herself adequately from a pregenital subjection to the mother as reflected in a powerful latent homosexuality, nor assert herself sufficiently in her identity as a woman to allow her to make a heterosexual object choice in the person of a man who was loved and desired. In her family, Tania was the youngest of three daughters; she was convinced that her parents had expected her to be a boy and had brought her up accordingly. She had few childhood memories and it seemed to me that her infantile past threw little light on her current pathology. When she was twelve, her parents had separated, leaving Tania alone with her mother, her elder sisters having already left home to go to university. She had later had difficulty in leaving her mother, whose favourite Tania thought she had been, but she was also very angry with her for having been a 'possessive, disparaged and disparaging' mother who was often depressed. As for her father, she experienced him as a seducer and avoided him, while confessing that she did have some feelings of longing towards him.

I immediately observed in the preliminary interviews that Tania was sometimes capable of genuine contact with me and of gaining access to feelings of sadness, symbolizing on the neurotic level. Sometimes, however, she would project; persecution feelings would then predominate, especially when she spoke of her personal or professional relations with the men she unconsciously envied. All the same, Tania in my opinion had sufficient introspective capacity for us to embark on the adventure of a psychoanalysis.

41

Risk of impasse

Transference of ambivalent feelings

For the first two years of the analysis, the transference was dominated by intense ambivalent feelings (love–hate) towards me. Tania came to her sessions punctually and paid me regularly, thereby showing that she valued me, but at the same time she took care to keep me at arm's length. For instance, she avoided addressing me directly as someone to whom she could express feelings of affection or rejection, sometimes telling me that for her a psychoanalyst ought to stay 'neutral' – which, in her mind, meant devoid of feelings and sexless.

However, while Tania seemed to ignore my presence and would not allow herself to be 'touched' affectively by my words, as if she were insensible and acting dead, it was nevertheless evident to me that she hated and appreciated me at one and the same time. Her transference affects, though, were regularly disavowed, projected and displaced on to other people in her circle. Whenever I tried to connect the feelings she attributed to other people by projection with the feelings she had in her relationship with me, Tania would simply interrupt my interpretations, either rejecting or ignoring them. In the early stages of her analysis, Tania had little access to the symbolic sense of verbal language and seldom brought her dreams, which were in any case mostly very short and accompanied by few associations. I also had the impression that she had largely lost the direct, genuine contact I had sensed in our first meetings, and that she was for the time being using me essentially for the purpose of discharging on to me the account of the disappointments and conflicts she encountered in her emotional and professional life – using me as a 'witness', rather than a 'party', to the transference, to borrow an expression from Paul Israël.

Despite this defensive distancing from any genuine consciousness of her transference affects and of the possibility of working through them in words, Tania nevertheless made progress in her everyday life. I noted, for example, that she had entered into a more lasting and less conflictual relationship with a man, and that she had accepted more responsibility in her job, albeit at the expense of intense anxieties, which we had been able to tackle and analyse. Whereas the patient's psychic conflicts were beginning to diminish as far as the external relationships in her day-to-day life were concerned, it became clear to me that these problems were increasingly becoming concentrated in her relationship with me and were intensifying – a frequent transference phenomenon in psychoanalysis. Moreover, it was this intensification of transference phenomena that I expected to initiate the process of insight and working through.

Working hypotheses awaiting confirmation

In view of the rarity of Tania's dreams, her lack of access to symbolization, and the importance of primitive defence mechanisms such as projective identification and omnipotence, I was unable to find my way through to her unconscious fantasies and to incorporate them in interpretations so that they could be worked through.

Pending the establishment of better communication between us on the symbolic verbal level, so that fruitful exchanges might ensue from my interpretations, I was, I felt, reduced to formulating provisional working hypotheses about the nature of her ambivalence and its repercussions on her relationship with me. For example, when Tania declared that she wanted a man at all costs, I presumed from the clinical material that this was not only so that she could blossom as a woman on the level of heterosexuality and genital psychosexuality, but that, at this stage of the analysis, it was more likely that she wanted to compete with the man in order to get close to him insidiously and to castrate him, thereby acting out her unconscious homosexual tendencies.

So I wondered: in what form was this situation now reproducing itself in Tania's relationship with me, unbeknown to either of us? On further reflection, I thought that this behaviour might perhaps be a form of unconscious revenge on the man with a view to getting rid of him, so that she could have her mother to herself, usurping her father's place. However, in turning back to her mother and identifying with her father, out of both guilt and the fear of confronting heterosexuality, was she once again overcome by the anxiety of being imprisoned in an exclusive homosexual relationship? In other words, I imagined that Tania must feel hemmed in between two opposing tendencies, between which she was unable to make a genuine choice. For when she moved ahead and confronted her heterosexual tendencies, the encounter with a man unleashed her persecutory retaliation anxieties that prevented her from working through her positive Oedipus complex; conversely, when she regressed, the homosexual attraction for her pregenital mother gave rise to claustrophobic anxieties bound up with the reversed Oedipus complex – the dilemma at the root of the central conflict in unconscious homosexuality, especially in women (J.-M. Quinodoz 1989). At this juncture in the analysis, I was waiting patiently for this unclear situation to be reproduced and for something new to arise in the transference relationship, whereby we could find a way round the blockage.

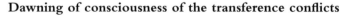

Dawning of consciousness of the transference conflicts

The unexpected threat of enactment

Our transference impasse burst into the light of day when Tania suddenly told me during one session that she would soon have no alternative to breaking off her analysis for lack of funds. This situation came entirely out of the blue for me, but I immediately felt that it heralded an enactment of unconscious trans-ference fantasies. The subsequent course of the session put me on the track of what she was trying to communicate to me through the lack of money.

I shall now give a more detailed account of the clinical material of the sessions. When I succeeded in demonstrating the unconscious reasons for the occurrence of this situation, a turning point in the analysis seemed to lie ahead. This change was confirmed by a dream that assumed particular signifi-cance in retrospect, offering as it did a key to the change that was taking place. This, for me, was a typical dream that turns over a page.

'I have not got the wherewithal'

When Tania told me that she was about to run out of funds and would have to break off her sessions before long, dozens of thoughts quickly passed through my mind. I was at first very surprised, because it had seemed to me that she had until then had the 'wherewithal', in terms of financial resources, to live in comfort while at the same time paying for her analysis herself. I then reflected on the unconscious psychosexual meaning that the relationship with money may assume in the transference, especially with female patients. For example, a woman's feeling of being 'poor' or 'broke' often proves to be an expression of the unconscious feeling of having been stripped of her female treasures in her relationship with her mother, as D. Quinodoz (1984) has shown. These ideas are based on Klein's work on the development of the early superego in girls and the persecutory anxiety associated with retaliation in the relationship with the mother:

> Because of the destructive tendencies once directed by her against the mother's body (or certain organs in it) and against the children in the womb, the girl anticipates retribution in the form of destruction of her own capacity for motherhood or of the organs connected with this function and of her own children.
>
> (Klein 1928: 194)

I have in fact observed similar manifestations in male patients in the analysis of their female parts.

These fantasies, connected with envy and destructiveness in relation to the mother's – the psychoanalyst's – womb are reflected in the transference in the form of the patient's sense of being impoverished by the psychoanalyst, representing her mother, and drained of her own capacity for motherhood. This internal situation is experienced as an insufficiency on both psychic and reality levels in a number of ways. Psychically, it may be felt as a lack of value and creativity, and in reality terms as an incapacity to produce children or a lack of financial resources. Conversely, and by projective identification on to the analyst, it also has the unconscious meaning that the patient sees her mother – the psychoanalyst – as stripped of value on the maternal and professional levels, because drained of her creative capacity by the daughter's destructive fantasies. In this situation, the transference confrontation arouses the unconscious persecutory feeling in the patient of being increasingly despoiled by her mother while, conversely, the daughter feels that her mother is giving her less and less. These conflicting forces may be enacted in the transference and the conflict is likely to persist for as long as it remains unconscious.

In the same session, Tania once again surprised me when she said that she was earning enough and was not short of money, but that she was spending it compulsively on things other than her analysis: 'If I am short of money to pay for my sessions,' Tania told me, 'it is because I am spending it on rubbish, on worthless things which are not even of any use to me . . . I simply can't help it!' Spontaneously realizing then that she was spending as much on these things as she paid me each month, Tania added: 'I sometimes tell myself that instead of buying rubbish, I ought instead to treat myself to something *to furnish and decorate my interior*, because *I am leaving the apartment my mother provided desperately empty*; at other times, though, *I feel that I have no right to give myself this pleasure.*'

Tania's words suddenly took on a profound symbolic value for me, because she was expressing ambivalence. On the one hand, by telling me that she was spending her money on 'rubbish', she was indirectly saying that what I was giving her as her analyst-mother was rubbish; but, on the other, she was expressing her sadness at being unable to make any use of her relationship with me, as a mother who could help her to 'furnish her interior' – that is, her woman's womb which she experienced as 'desperately empty', feeling guilty as she did at her unconscious attacks on her mother's womb, and the victim of her mother's retaliation.

I then told her that, by coming to analysis, she presumably expected to find in me a mother who was female enough to arouse in her the wish to 'furnish and decorate her interior' – that is, her 'womanly interior provided by her mother', a woman's womb that she was leaving 'desperately empty'. However, deep down she was engaged in a violent struggle with me: driven by obsessive energy, she was disparaging my work with her in the same way as her own capacity to work with – me as the representative of a mother both envied by and envious of her daughter. This was presumably what she was trying to tell me by spending her money on 'rubbish', so that she felt more and more impoverished and despoiled by me, her psychoanalyst-mother. I added that, apart from this, she felt that she did have the financial 'wherewithal' to continue her analysis, just as a daughter feels that she has the potential to become a woman like her mother.

Tania listened to me in silence, but with unaccustomed attention, and seemed to grasp the symbolic meaning of my interpretations. She made just one comment, which I saw as a sign that she had understood me: 'I never felt that I was seen as a woman, either by my mother or by my father. After my sisters were born, my parents waited a long time for a boy, and my arrival disappointed them. How could I get myself out of that?'

In the ensuing sessions, I saw that her changed attitude towards me was persisting. At the end of the month she brought me my fee without talking about it. She seemed more collaborative and receptive in our exchanges, and less sure of herself and authoritarian than usual. She had added a feminine touch to her clothing, whereas in general she would dress in grey and her style was more masculine. She no longer spoke of breaking off her analysis, but did not spontaneously take up the content of the various interpretations I had given her in the previous session. She confirmed my impression that our relationship was in the process of changing when, shortly afterwards, she declared to me: 'I am fed up with sadomasochistic relationships!' This brief statement came like a flash of insight and represented the beginnings of a positive response to my attempts to interpret her sadism towards me in the transference – a sadism that she turned back on herself in the form of masochism and enactment. It was indeed the first time that Tania had shown any consciousness of the latent sadomasochism that played such an important part in her.

Notwithstanding these hesitant signs of progress, Tania continued to supply relatively little associative material to allow me to proceed further with this incipient process of elaboration.

A dream that turns over a page

A highly significant dream

A week later, in the context of the barely perceptible changes I had detected, Tania brought me a dream. At a stroke, its content represented in an enormous fresco the central unconscious fantasies underlying Tania's pathology, with a clarity and coherence unprecedented in her analysis. What surprised me was how the dream contained visual representations of the basic elements of the ambivalent transference situation in which she had engaged, with psychosexual references to her infantile past, as if drawn in a picture or map. I was all the more astonished by this dream, whose main feature was its staging of the underlying conflict of rivalry with me as the representative of the father, because it came at the very point when Tania was in the process of resolving the impasse that had resulted from the unconscious conflict with me-as-her-mother.

'I have had a horrible dream,' she told me. 'It began pleasantly enough, but turned more and more ghastly. Only a mad person could dream anything like

46

that! I was going out to catch a bus. But instead of catching the one in the direction I wanted to go in, I got into another bus that was going the other way. I did not realize it immediately, but the woman driver told me that my ticket was not valid for this destination. So I got off at the next stop and took a bus in the direction I had first wanted to go in. I sat down, and then, through the window, I saw a man I liked and I smiled at him. To my surprise, the unknown man gestured to me, got into the bus and sat down opposite me. I was pleased but worried, because he attracted me. But the situation suddenly changed into a frightening science-fiction scene: he and I were dressed in airtight space suits, he was standing in front of me and I saw him draw a laser gun and aim it at me. To avoid him, I threw myself to the ground and acted dead. Without suspecting anything, he approached, and when he was very near, I grabbed his weapon and shot him. It was unbearable, because I wanted and did not want to kill him at one and the same time – so I fired only to neutralize him . . . I went away leaving him lying there wounded.'

Uncanny, anxious feelings

'You have to be crazy to dream something like that! I wouldn't dare tell it to anyone! It was a sexual theme, yet it did not seem sexual . . . In the science-fiction scene, it is the woman who is at first the victim of the man, but then she is the one who grabs the gun and threatens to kill him. Have I reversed the roles? Is it the conflict I am having with you here, because I think the man in the dream is you . . .?' Tania said. 'Why does the relationship always end up going wrong when I am attracted to a man?' she added, with a note of genuine sadness that indicated that she was beginning to feel that a dream could have a deep transference meaning, casting light simultaneously on past and present, and opening up prospects for the future.

I myself was impressed by the violence of the dream content and by how Tania involved me in it. At the same time I admired the way the dream content displayed with unparalleled clarity the different levels of Tania's ambivalence, with respect both to her sadistic and to her reparative drives. It was precisely this characteristic – of illustrating in a huge fresco the organization of the drives, unconscious fantasies and defences – that suggested to me that such dreams result from the 'return' to the ego, in the process of integration, of previously disavowed, split-off and projected parts, which can subsequently undergo repression.

Fear of going backwards

After a silence, Tania went on: 'How could I have such a disturbing dream just when I felt that I was getting somewhere through my analysis . . . Is that the way the situation is developing in the unconscious too? This dream suggests that it is in fact the opposite that is happening. I seem to be retreating instead of making progress!' Thus Tania was simultaneously expressing her intuition of the changes she had perceived in herself and the fear that the anxiety-inducing primitive content of this dream might merely mean that she was relapsing into an impasse. I have often observed such contradictory feelings, made up of both relief and anxiety, accompanying such dreams.

'Do you think I shall get myself out of it one day?' Tania then asked me, manifestly more and more disturbed and anxious. I felt that the anxiety was in the process of gaining the upper hand and that, before attempting to analyse the dream contents proper, I would have to address myself first to the point of urgency, the point where the anxiety seemed to me to be keenest: 'If you have been able to have a dream that throws light on various aspects of what is happening between you and me, might it be a sign that you have become capable of representing to yourself these unknown, hitherto secret parts of yourself?' I enumerated the various aspects of her defences, pointing out what she was defending against and by what means: 'For example,' I said, 'the action of this dream seems to demonstrate what happens when you are attracted by a man; could it be that desire immediately gives way to envy of his sex, so that you feel that the only way you can protect yourself is to attack this man who you feel is attacking you? That is why a love scene is transformed into a destructive one in which you grab his "gun" – symbolically representing his penis – so as to get rid of him . . .'

Caught between heterosexual and homosexual tendencies

Tania said: 'I find it hard to believe that this dream is not a sign of a retreat.' She then brought a precious association: 'In the dream, the buses remind me of the ones I catch to go and see my mother or my father, because since their divorce they have been living at opposite ends of town. The first bus took me towards the place where my mother lives, and its terminus is named after a female virgin martyr saint. But I got the direction wrong because I wanted to go the other way, to the place where my father, who has remarried, lives.' This to me was not a simple contrast between going to see her mother or going to see her father, but indicated a choice between a regressive fusional relationship with a pregenital mother, which would give rise to homosexual persecution feelings, and progress in the direction of the couple comprising the genital parents, accompanied by the persecutory anxieties aroused by this confrontation. The dream thus presented the terms of a choice.

I responded: 'Your dream is contributing something new because it shows two possible directions and that you have a choice between turning back and going forward. For example, I have the impression that the first bus is travelling

48

in the direction of an exclusive relationship with your mother, which would turn you away from men and from your wish to create a couple, so that you would be liable to remain a "virgin and martyr". On the other hand, when you choose your father's direction – the direction shown on the ticket – might that confront you not only with your father but also with the couple he represents, as well as with your own femininity and the hope of meeting a man you could love and desire?'

Tania at first protested vehemently: 'I *hate* you. I have been in a comfortable position here for a long time, as if I were alone with my mother, and you want to drive me out of it! That is not what I came here for!' Then, calming down: 'I do believe what I just told you, but at the same time I don't really believe it, because this dream has made me realize how I often hesitate when faced with a choice and am tempted to go into reverse. I am afraid of going mad if I go on avoiding making a choice!' This change in the tone of Tania's affects was unexpected and surely represented a turning point, in the sense of a diminution of projective mechanisms and a genuine insight into her conflict with her father and with men, as well as into the couple in a context of love and genital sexuality.

Conflict with the mother is followed in the transference by conflict with the father

After a silence, Tania went on to ask herself whether she had sometimes acted dead in my presence, as in the dream: 'I wonder if I have acted dead for a long time here and am in the process of waking up . . .' She added: 'I realize that I am changing: I am getting closer to my father and I feel less apprehension towards men.' Then, after a further silence, she remembered her first reaction after telling me the dream: 'I immediately thought it was a sexual scene . . . And then I said to myself: am I reversing the roles? Instead of a victim, am I becoming the aggressor? Why do I grab the man's weapon and threaten to kill him – to kill *you*? Why did I dream that I was doing such horrible things to you?'

I told her that, in the dream, she was showing first of all that she had decided not to go back to her mother but had chosen to go to her father: might the reason have been that she wanted to remain 'a virgin and martyr', to turn away from a man and give up her own femininity, feeling herself to be the victim of both her mother and her father? I thought that the reinforcement of her heterosexual tendencies had been accompanied by a reduction in the influence of her latent homosexual tendencies. However, the awakening of her wish to go to her father and the meeting with the unknown man transformed the scene: Tania acted dead in order to attract this man so that she could neutralize him. 'Might that be how you imagine a sexual relationship – a reversal of the sexes in which the woman grabs the man's penis so as to get rid of him?'

Retrospective illumination

I then suggested a parallel between the content of the dream and the transference situation, telling her that she had presumably 'acted dead' in my presence for a long time, as if she imagined us to be protected in our insulating suits, so as to avoid feeling herself to be a woman in relation to me as the representative not only of her mother but also of her father and of her parental couple. For example, when she had found herself short of money to pay me, was it only out of envy of her mother's treasures? Or was it also in relation to me, representing her father, so that she could grab the money owed to me as if it were a symbolic virile force – the laser gun – which she could then turn on me and avoid the confrontation with the man? By reversing the roles in this way, was she perhaps in an impasse, unable to achieve satisfaction either in her usurped male goals or in her legitimate female ones?

Tania: 'I acknowledge that I did not dare admit to myself that my father had a good side, and that he sometimes intervened to stop me losing myself in my mother. But then, rather than admitting to myself that I was sensually attracted by him, I would get angry with him and see him as a seducer, and since his presence made me feel uncomfortable, I then ignored him and shut myself away.'

Myself: 'So you were already acting dead with him, as you have done with me?'

Tania: 'Yes, so that he could not reach me.'

Myself: 'In this way you were depriving him of the opportunity to play his part as a father who loved you, and at the same time you, his daughter, were depriving yourself of the pleasure of having a father and loving him?'

Tania: 'One day I was feeling sad and my father came up to me to comfort me: I don't know what came over me, but I hit him and ran away and took refuge with my mother; I was ashamed of what I had done, but I did not show any of it.'

Myself: 'Perhaps it was the same as in the dream: might you have acted dead to allow him to come close, and then hit him – castrated him – in the same way as you have often done with men, by attracting them and frustrating them, and as you often do with my interpretations here?'

Tania: 'It's true, I used to provoke my father, I bashed him one, and then I took refuge with my mother. I remember him looking at me sadly; he seemed disappointed.' In the transference relationship, she had almost subjected me to a similar fate by threatening to break off her analysis, and she often consigned my interpretations to the same fate by unconsciously seeing them as 'rubbish' (in the mother transference) and by making them sterile (in the father transference).

Myself: 'Hasn't the same thing often happened here, when you seemed not to hear me? And then you would make a caustic comment that nullified my

50

words – in particular, the ones which had touched you most and which you had secretly appreciated without showing your emotion?'

Tania: 'I know, I do it against my own will.'

An incipient process of reparation

I have deliberately reproduced the expression 'I do it against my own will' because it illustrates how Tania was beginning to become conscious of her aggressive feelings and destructiveness towards me. At the same time, however, there was evidence of a wish to take care of herself and of me, with the nascent aim of reparation, and so I said to her: 'It is *against* your will that a part of you has *done* things that threatened to break off our relationship – for example, when you thought you could no longer afford to pay me. But there is also another side that feels *good will* towards me, because, in the dream, did you not try to spare me?' By adding this, I was indicating to her that, by continuing to come to her sessions and to pay for them, she was in the process of integrating her affects of love and hate and of overcoming her ambivalence.

At this point I shall break off my account of the most significant moments in these analytic sessions, an account that falls far short of a full description of the rich complexity of the work of elaborating a dream of this kind. Extensive further development would be needed to demonstrate even more precisely the clarity and coherence with which this dream illuminated the unconscious fantasies underlying the organization of this patient's conflicts as expressed in the transference. However, that would take us too far. Instead, I shall end this narrative with a few words about the development of our relationship in the ensuing months.

Transformations in Tania's dreams

Through integration, splitting gives way to repression

The analysis of this dream that turned over a page marked the resumption of a slow process of working through that was gradually accomplished during the course of the next few months. I observed how repression gradually replaced primitive defence mechanisms as Tania's psychic functioning increasingly entered into a symbolic and neurotic register. These psychic changes were accompanied by dreams whose structure seemed to me to be closer to that of classical dreams, including as they did representations of unsatisfied repressed wishes in a context of better-integrated relations with more whole and less partial objects. I shall give an example in Chapter 9. The succession of her dreams during this period of analysis reflected a process of working through at a deep level in the transference, connected in particular with a better integration of her ambivalence, a strengthening of her heterosexual tendencies and an increased trust in the value of her female capacities.

For example, I noticed a significant change in Tania's affects when I heard her utter the word 'love' for the first time: 'The man I am now sharing my life with – I feel that I can love him.' At the same time I observed in her the emergence of incestuous oedipal wishes that had hitherto been repressed and disavowed, whose transference meaning it took her quite a time to perceive. This was illustrated by a dream in which she was disputing her mother's right to ownership of the 'family jewels' inherited from her grandmother: 'I told my mother: now it's my turn to have the jewels; they were passed on to you from generation to generation with instructions to wear them only at a wedding!' This dream was followed by another that indicated the guilt she felt at making use of her jewels, the symbol of her femininity, in which she represented herself as a prostitute: 'I was walking in the street when my handbag opened and I dropped my jewels into the gutter; at first I did not dare look for them, but I overcame my disgust and picked them up before they disappeared down the drain. I was relieved . . .'

This development was not unaccompanied by major fluctuations in her ambivalence and by alternation between phases of advance and phases of retreat. For instance, the appearance of a conscious wish to have a child momentarily reinforced her ambivalent affects as well as her latent homosexual tendencies, as reflected in ambiguous statements such as: 'I should like to get married soon so that *my husband can have a child* . . .' What did she mean? Did she want *him* to carry in his womb a child whose father *she* would be – in a reversed Oedipus complex – or was Tania in fact expressing her wish *herself* to bear a child in her womb of which *he* would be the father – in a direct Oedipus complex?

This recurrence of ambivalence – between her rekindled unconscious homosexual tendencies and her heterosexual tendencies – led to a recurrence of anxiety, which we were able to analyse in the light of earlier dreams, such as the one about the buses travelling in opposite directions. Through a strengthening of her heterosexual tendencies, Tania gradually became increasingly conscious of her wish to have a child with me in the transference at symbolic level: 'I realize that, when I want to have a child and am disappointed at not having one yet, it is also with you that I want to have one: doesn't a successful analysis mean wanting to have a child with you in imagination?' she said, 'but such an idea seemed to me for a long time to be intolerably criminal . . .' Tania had gradually succeeded in tolerating, and putting into words, incestuous sexual desires towards me. Moreover, she was expressing them in an affective register in which love was becoming stronger than hate; this contrasted with the situation prior to our embarking on the adventure of a psychoanalysis, in which hate, sadism, violence and intense destructiveness had dominated her fantasies, dreams and relationships.

PART THREE

Dreams and integration

8

Investigations in the
psychoanalytic literature

Similar but different dreams

Searching the psychoanalytic literature to find out whether such dreams had been discussed by other authors before me, I found only a small number of observations that were wholly consistent with my description of dreams that turn over a page. I could not discover a single example in Freud, although his work includes references to the relations between dreams, anxiety and psychosis which are relevant to the formation of these dreams. The closest approach to dreams that turn over a page is probably to be found in Arieti (1963), to whose contribution my attention was drawn by Blechner (2000) after the publication of my paper (J.-M. Quinodoz 1999). Although Freud, Ferenczi, Winnicott and Grinberg all mention anxiety dreams which at the same time possess an elaborative function, these references are general rather than specifically relevant to our subject. It is mainly in Segal (1988 and 1991), Guillaumin (1979) and Stewart (1973, 1981 and 1992) that I came across descriptions of dreams with similar characteristics to my own observations, although differing in a number of respects. However, my investigations are not exhaustive and further research is called for. I would add here that, in the Internet discussion of my paper on the website of the *International Journal of Psycho-Analysis*, several colleagues contributed examples from analytic practice that confirmed the clinical value of my observations (Williams 1999). Various personal communications from other analysts also proved valuable, because even with today's sophisticated search facilities, information about a concept that as yet lacks a specific definition was hard to come by.

Dreams, anxiety and splitting of the ego in Freud

Anxiety dreams: Satisfaction for the id and anxiety for the ego

In 1938 Freud discussed the issue of anxiety dreams. He noted that, because they have an unpleasant content and awaken the dreamer, they seemingly contradict his thesis that a dream is always a wish fulfilment: after all, it may be objected, anxiety cannot be the fulfilment of a wish. Freud disposes of this objection by asserting that every dream is the product of a conflict, a rule to which even anxiety dreams are no exception: 'Something that is a satisfaction for the unconscious id may for that very reason be a cause of anxiety for the ego' (Freud 1940a [1938]: 170–1).

This observation is in my view applicable to dreams that turn over a page. On the one hand, the regressive content of such a dream may be deemed to correspond to the satisfaction of a wish from the unconscious id, thus opening up the 'royal road' to a knowledge of the dreamer's unconscious and the possibility of working it through. On the other hand, in the case of splitting, this regressive content may at the same time be regarded as a threat to the integrity of the dreamer's ego, which triggers an alarm signal in the form of sensations of anxiety (ibid.: 199).

Anxiety, repressed contents and disavowed contents

My contention that the dreamer's anxiety corresponds more to a disavowed, split-off content than to one that is repressed is borne out by another of Freud's observations, in which he draws a parallel between the anxiety stemming from repression and that due to a fragment of rejected reality:

> There [in neurosis] we see that a reaction of anxiety sets in whenever the repressed instinct makes a thrust forward, and that the outcome of the conflict is only a compromise and does not provide complete satisfaction. Probably *in a psychosis the rejected piece of reality constantly forces itself upon the mind, just as the repressed instinct does in a neurosis*, and that is why in both cases the consequences too are the same.
>
> (Freud 1924e: 186, my emphasis)

Note that Freud is here making a crucial distinction between an anxiety of the ego when it is confronted with repressed contents (an anxiety of neurotic origin) and an ego anxiety resulting from 'a piece of rejected reality' – that is to say, from disavowed and split-off contents as he was shortly to conceptualize them (anxiety in the psychotic register).

Splitting of the ego in psychosis and neurosis

From the concept of splitting of the ego, initially defined as a characteristic of psychosis, Freud was eventually to conclude that splitting of the ego took place not only in psychosis but also in neurosis – an idea that is still by no means universally accepted by psychoanalysts. Hence the predominant organization of the personality results from the relations between the psychotic and non-psychotic parts of the personality, in terms of their relative strength, as Freud had already discovered in connection with the splitting of the ego:

> Two psychical attitudes have been formed instead of a single one – one, the normal one, which takes account of reality, and another which under the influence of instincts detaches the ego from reality. The two exist alongside of each other. The issue depends on their relative strength. If the second is or becomes the stronger, the necessary precondition for a psychosis is present. If the relation is reversed, then there is an apparent cure of the delusional disorder.
>
> (Freud 1940a [1938]: 202)

The idea of the splitting of the ego observed by Freud in both psychosis and neurosis is taken a step further in the distinction between the psychotic and non-psychotic parts of the personality (Bion 1957).

Freudian ideas that are still by no means fully accepted

The reason for my insistence on these postulates is that they are seen to underlie a conception of psychic functioning based not merely on repression, as in the first part of Freud's oeuvre, but also on mechanisms connected with psychosis, such as the disavowal of reality and the splitting of the ego, which he described later. These psychic mechanisms were subsequently to lead to the development of Klein's concepts of primitive defences and of integration, upon which my own hypotheses are substantially grounded. Moreover, the discussions of my ideas about dreams that turn over a page have shown me that many psycho-analysts today still analyse dreams mainly in accordance with a repression-based conception of psychic functioning, so that phenomena associated with inte-gration are not taken sufficiently into account. This indicates that Lacan's focus on neurotic mechanisms has remained a powerful influence on French-language psychoanalysis to this day (J.-M. Quinodoz 2000c). These positions tend to overshadow not only some of Freud's decisive contributions subsequent to the metapsychological papers of 1915, but also the important Kleinian and post-Kleinian developments they inspired, which in my view are highly relevant to the psychopathology of dreams that turn over a page.

Post-Freudian contributions

Ferenczi: Traumatic dreams and the elaborative function

Like dreams that turn over a page, Ferenczi's notion of the traumatic dream involves paradox, because these dreams perform an elaborative function despite their anxiety-inducing content. Ferenczi attributes trauma to the paradoxical effect on the mind of sexual wishes that cannot be fulfilled – a potentially traumatic situation that can arise in anxiety dreams. Such dreams, according to Ferenczi, have two inseparable aspects: the 'primary dream', which is a pure repetition of the trauma, and the 'secondary dream', which is a partial attempt to overcome the trauma by means of a 'narcissistic split' (1931: 241–2). The conception of traumatic dreams thus resembles that of dreams that turn over a page in that, notwithstanding their anxiety-inducing content, they possess an elaborative function.

Moreover, the concepts of splitting, projection and even projective identification are also inherent in these dreams, as Ferenczi notes in connection with a clinical example: '[. . .] the mechanism of projection as the result of the narcissistic split is also represented in the displacement of the events from herself on to "a girl"' (ibid.: 242). Finally, in his view that the therapeutic effect of traumatic dreams results from a 'trance' that brings about the reliving of the 'sensory impressions' rediscovered in the 'secondary dream', thereby continuing the working through of the traumatic contents, Ferenczi comes close to the ideas of integration and working through that are applicable to the dreams I describe. His conception thus opens up a field of research that has been further explored by many psychoanalysts – including Garma (1970), for whom traumatic dreams are hallucinations of masked traumatic situations seen as determined solely by the mechanism of repression. Although much more could be said about the relations between dreams with traumatic content and dreams that turn over a page, such a consideration would exceed the bounds I have set myself.

Winnicott's 'healing' dreams

In his paper on hate in the countertransference, Winnicott (1947) refers briefly to certain personal dreams that he calls 'healing' dreams. He associates them with stages in his personal analysis and self-analysis: 'Incidentally I would add that during my analysis and in the years since the end of my analysis I have had a long series of these healing dreams which, although in many cases unpleasant, have each one of them marked my arrival at a new stage in emotional development' (p.197). In this paper Winnicott notes that these healing dreams have often helped him to clear up countertransference difficulties. He gives the example of a dream that aroused particular anxiety which he had on experiencing difficulty with a psychotic woman patient who irritated him and disorganized his thought. It was a dream of fragmentation of parts of his body, and Winnicott points out that, because he had been able to remember and analyse this dream with its primitive content, he had then succeeded in overcoming his countertransference reactions: 'Whatever other interpretations might be made in respect of this dream the result of my having dreamed it and remembered it was that I was able to take up this analysis again and even to heal the harm done to it by my irritability' (ibid.: 198). Yet Winnicott does not seem to have developed further his idea of the 'healing' dream, which in my view closely resembles the phenomena subsumed by me in the notion of 'dreams that turn over a page'.

Arieti: Criteria of improvement and the dreams of schizophrenics

Arieti (1963) describes a hallucination-like dream observed by him in phases of improvement in the symptoms of schizophrenic patients. This author here deems such dreams – whose characteristics bear a strong resemblance to those I have seen in dreams that turn over a page – to be a valid criterion of change in a patient. He gives the following concise description:

> There is a characteristic which is especially important in alerting us that great changes towards improvement are made: the changing aspect of dreams. The dreams of recovering patients acquire a particular content which may be interpreted adversely by therapists with little experience with psychotic patients. Unexpectedly the content deals with material which seems very similar to the delusional material, which appeared during the acute or active phase of the illness. The patient, however, in the dream now finds solutions to these conflicts.
>
> (Arieti 1963: 26)

Arieti's description is thus in many respects consistent with my own observations on dreams that turn over a page. For instance, the type of dream he describes arises in the clinical context of a symptomatic improvement in a patient who has been through a psychotic episode (a delusion), which is then followed by a significant dream whose primitive fantasy content corresponds to that of the no longer extant psychotic episode. Arieti adds that the particular content of such dreams is liable to be interpreted unfavourably if the therapist lacks experience with psychotic patients. He emphasizes that the dream brings a solution to the dreamer's intrapsychic conflicts.

Arieti does not develop his theoretical views on dreams of this type further, but illustrates them by a clinical example, which I shall now summarize. The patient was a 23-year-old woman who had come to New York and was living with a man very different from the conservative southern people among whom she had been brought up. One day she was found screaming in the street in a psychotic state. When hospitalized, she was hallucinating and delusional, imagining that the Russians had invaded the city and were chasing her. When the patient's condition subsequently improved, it was discovered that the episode had been triggered by a letter from her parents announcing that they were coming to visit her in New York. Her panic at the idea that her parents would discover the kind of life she was living, in particular with this man, induced a delusion in her in which the Russians, who represented her parents, were invading the city and chasing her. The patient recovered from her delusion in a few weeks.

A year later, a dream indicated that a more significant change had taken place: the patient dreamed that she was being chased by her parents all over New York City. Arieti notes that in this dream 'there is an attempt to solve problems at a much less unrealistic level', and adds that such a 'patient no longer tries to deal with his conflicts in an openly psychotic way, but in that psychotic way which is physiologic and available to every human being: the dream-world' (ibid.: 27).

This paper is relevant to our subject in a number of respects. The first concerns the features shared by the dreams described by Arieti with dreams that turn over a page. A second reason is that Arieti describes the occurrence of such dreams in schizophrenic patients, thus confirming the role of primitive defence mechanisms in their formation. However, in his description of the kinds of psychotic functioning involved, Arieti resorts to a neurotically based, ego-psychology type of theory of psychic functioning and dreams. Apart from the role of the loss of the perception of reality, he essentially invokes 'fixations, repressions, defenses, etc.' (ibid.: 28), and in my view does not adequately distinguish between the mature defence mechanisms characteristic of neurosis and the primitive ones that belong to the realm of psychosis.

Blechner: Borderline patients and their dreams

In a paper on changes in the dreams of borderline patients in psychoanalysis, Blechner (1983) describes a type of dream that accompanies progress in the treatment, but whose content paradoxically becomes increasingly complex and strange. In this author's view, the dreams of borderline patients show a development during the course of analysis, but cannot be understood solely in terms of classical theory. These dreams initially have a very factual narrative structure, presenting events in the manner of a newspaper report; they also lack the typical illogicality and bizarreness of ordinary dreams. With the progress of the treatment, the dreams of borderline patients gradually take on the same character as those of neurotics, eventually becoming 'more "psychotic" in structure' (p. 489), exhibiting bizarreness, sudden shifts, and so on. Blechner attributes these changes to the acquisition by the patient of a better capacity for symbolic representation; without explicitly referring to the concepts of disavowal and splitting of the ego, he postulates that, in a borderline patient, 'the psyche defends its capacity to see the world reasonably by sheltering such representations in the dream life' (ibid.: 497). In a later communication, Blechner (2000) connects such dreams with the ones described by me, thus partly confirming my views (J.-M. Quinodoz 2000a).

He illustrates these changes by the example of a woman patient, the first dream in whose analysis expressed a reaction of drawing physically close to her analyst, which was the very antithesis of her overt distancing attitude towards him. Later in the analysis, the analyst was to discover that the physical and mental proximity which the patient so yearned for – and expressed in her dream – in fact constituted a source of dissociative and delusional anxiety. In my view, this inaugural dream possesses a paradoxical character like that of a dream that turns over a page, in that it presents a content that subsequently proves psychotic and a simultaneous wish for reparation – that is, the wish to recover her psychotic part with a view to integrating it better.

Grinberg: Evacuative, elaborative and mixed dreams

The fact that dreams that turn over a page indicate progress despite their regressive content puts us in mind of the 'mixed dreams' described by Grinberg (1967 and 1987). This author distinguishes three types of dreams, namely evacuative, elaborative and mixed dreams, of which the last combines aspects of the first two. Evacuative dreams present a primitive content and have the aim of expelling ill-tolerated contents into an internal or external object that serves as a container. Elaborative dreams belong to the depressive position and coincide with phases of integration, signifying for Grinberg a mutative stage in the patient's psychic processes: 'These dreams appear at the most advanced stages of the analysis and seem to constitute a "marker" connected with an important internal change' (1967: 763).

On the basis of Grinberg's distinctions, dreams that turn over a page may be regarded as falling within the group of mixed dreams, containing as they do both evacuative and integrative elements. However, in dreams that turn over a page, the primitive anxiety-inducing aspects are not evacuated as they are in mixed dreams; on the contrary, they contribute to the reintegration of the ego by virtue of their integrative trend, and it is in my view precisely their reintegration that becomes a momentary source of anxiety for the dreamer.

In a paper on the termination entitled 'Sweating it out', Segal (1988) presents a number of dreams of a male patient that resemble dreams that turn over a page in certain respects – in particular, the fact that they were frightening regressive dreams that occurred at the end of the patient's analysis, when he had achieved a better degree of integration. He suffered from disintegration anxieties and profuse sweating – hence the paper's title – and had had temporary hallucinations, which disappeared during the analysis. As the termination approached, he had a series of anxiety-inducing dreams – in particular, a nightmare in which he was suffering from hallucinations. Notwithstanding the primitive, anxiety-inducing nature of the dream content, Segal stood by her decision to terminate the analysis, considering that the patient had manifestly arrived at a better degree of integration in other respects. In particular, he was now able to *dream* that he was having a hallucination instead of actually *having* it – a sign of progress and a new-found capacity for symbolization.

The main relevant dream in Segal's patient occurred just before the termination, and its frightening content had revived the old fears of the patient – who was a scientist – that he was mentally deficient; however, the analysis of this dream was followed by great relief and a definite improvement. The patient dreamed that his son was a mutilated baby who was only a mouth and could not be fed. He had no senses – no sight, no hearing, not even a sense of touch. As the dream had come after the analyst had been away for a week, she considered that, when the analyst had gone away, a major part of the patient had gone with her, representing his mother as she did, and that the mutilated baby represented the patient deprived of his senses:

> In this dream he [the patient] came back to the most violent and primitive projective identification in which he put into me his sense organs, his insides, and left himself mentally deficient and unable to introject – he could not be fed.
>
> (Segal 1988: 171–2)

This dream rekindled the fear the patient had had at the beginning of his analysis that he was mentally deficient and mad. Notwithstanding the recurrence of these anxieties, the analysis of the dream revealed that the patient was capable of working through regressive aspects of himself, so that he recovered the capacity for feeling and thinking that he had for a long time projected on to his analyst. This was borne out in the ensuing sessions, when the patient reported to the analyst a number of positive developments in his life – in particular, the fact that he had succeeded in finishing a scientific paper that was important for his work, which he had previously thought he would never be able to write.

Regarding the case history presented in 'Sweating it out', Segal makes three points relevant to dreams that turn over a page. First, she notes that the termination often brings back to the surface ancient themes, reawakens anxieties and remobilizes past defences, but does not necessarily involve the reappearance of symptoms, as Freud had believed. The termination is a period of working through that is sometimes extremely painful; in this example of oversensitivity to separation, we see how the patient eventually resigned himself to facing the solitude-related anxieties bound up with separation and death, and to leaving his analyst.

Second, Segal draws attention to the countertransference difficulty presented by such dreams to the psychoanalyst, in particular when they come at the end of the analysis. When such a dream coincides with the termination, it is in her view not necessarily a token of regression, although not everyone shares this opinion:

> Some may think that a patient who has such primitive fantasies and defenses and resists so much the ending is not ready to stop. That was what my patient often tried to make me think. I had few doubts that this decision was right.
>
> (ibid.: 173)

Third, Segal enquires as to the criteria to be used by the analyst to justify his decision to terminate the analysis despite the reappearance of dreams and primitive fantasies of the kind the patient had exhibited at the beginning of his analysis and subsequently abandoned. She adduces a number of structural criteria, which she invokes in her evaluation, such as a sufficient degree of progress from the paranoid-schizoid position – in which splitting, projective identification and fragmentation predominate – towards the depressive position; a better capacity for relating to external and internal objects; increased toleration of conflict and separation; and better internalization of good experiences. However, Segal notes that the depressive position is never completely resolved, and that fluctuations persist throughout life:

> The assessment has to be about the severity and persistence of bad states of mind. In this patient the fact of ending reawakened the most primitive of fantasies and defenses. But the situation was very different from that at the beginning of his analysis. The symptoms were minimal and the regressions were mostly contained in dreams, fantasies and the sessions. [. . .] Whereas in the past he had acted out in relationships and symptoms, he could now tolerate the knowledge of disturbing parts of himself. He had internalized sufficiently a good analytic experience to reestablish good internal objects and to internalize the psychoanalytic function of self-awareness.
>
> (ibid.: 174)

In *Dream, Art, Phantasy* (Segal 1991), the author mentions a similar dream in an analysand who had had hallucination-like mental states (for example, he felt that he had a motor-cycle in his head). These symptoms disappeared two years later when he was able to *dream* that he was having hallucinations. However, Segal points out, this does not mean that the dream cured him magically; it was 'the integration and assimilation of the insights acquired' in the analytic work that made it possible for a dream rather than a hallucination to arise (p. 40).

Segal's observations thus substantially conform to mine, in particular in her view that anxiety dreams may occur during the termination phase as a result of the patient's progress in acquiring the capacity to symbolize. My reason for verbalizing this change by explicitly interpreting it to the patient in an initial stage is to take advantage of this newly acquired capacity for representation, as shown earlier. Again, although Segal's contribution concentrates on the period leading up to the end of the analysis, her reference to structural criteria enables us to apply her ideas to a wider context and to consider such anxiety-inducing dreams as corresponding to a phase of integration at any point in the psychoanalytic process, as I have also noted, and not only at termination.

Guillaumin: 'Recapitulative dreams'

The concept of 'recapitulative' or 'synthesizing dreams' was introduced by Guillaumin (1979) to highlight certain dreams that are more striking than others because they clearly portray a sequence of episodes that recapitulate the dreamer's basic conflicts while at the same time offering an active solution to them. The clarity of these dreams results from the fact that they reveal 'the subject's most important and fundamental problems' (p. 106), illuminating both the past and the future of the dreamer's defensive organization, especially in the context of the transference, and thus considerably facilitating the psychoanalyst's task of interpretation.

The clarity and coherence with which the underlying unconscious transference conflicts are revealed by recapitulative dreams – more precisely than by ordinary dreams – are reminiscent of the clarity and coherence that impress me in connection with dreams that turn over a page. For instance, Guillaumin draws attention to a number of characteristics of the dreams he describes, and in particular to their chronology, which exhibits 'a dialectical progression in defence, which follows an ascending genetic order (in the direction of development)' (p. 105) – a temporal organization that subsequently proves to be a faithful reflection of the dreamer's psychic organization. This author considers the dream to possess an organizing activity that follows 'the line of a certain history that appears to be genuinely the subject's' (p. 107), in which the activity of the 'dream ego' opens the way to that of the 'waking ego'.

Being particularly concerned to examine various theoretical and clinical aspects of dreams' recapitulative power (the diachronic dimension), Guillaumin does not dwell on the conditions for their occurrence, as I have done with regard to dreams that turn over a page – an approach that enabled me to study the primitive mechanisms thereby involved (the synchronic dimension). However, on reading Guillaumin's second clinical example, I was struck by the fact that he describes a number of aspects shared by dreams that turn over a page. For example, the recapitulative dream mentioned was an anxiety-inducing dream that came 'after a period of change' (p. 105) which proved to be the starting point for a 'subsequent oedipal development' (ibid., note 1). As to the regressive dream content, the author notes that it induced so much anxiety that it woke the patient, who felt 'very excited and anxious' (p. 104).

Finally, when Guillaumin seeks to develop a theory of recapitulative dreams, he is seen to invoke a conception of the psychical apparatus in which the neurotic model of ego organization predominates, involving a whole ego and based on repression. Although seemingly setting little store by the role of primitive defences such as, in particular, splitting, Guillaumin nevertheless senses that they too are relevant, noting explicitly that the diminution of splitting is not unconnected with the occurrence of his patient's dream, even if he does not develop the clinical and theoretical implications: 'It [the dream] appeared after a period of change in which the analysand was gradually abandoning a rigid split' (p. 103).

In a recent discussion of the concept of dreams that turn over a page, Guillaumin (personal communication) expresses the view that recapitulative dreams reflect mainly the diachronic aspect of dream activity, whereas the type of dream I describe places more emphasis on its synchronic aspect. Although I myself have so far concentrated more on the synchronic dimension, Guillaumin's comment indicates to me that synchronic and diachronic aspects in fact coexist in dreams that turn over a page: the synchronic aspect may be seen as corresponding to the phase of recovery of the split-off parts of the ego, while the diachronic aspect correlates with the emergence of unconscious fantasies when repression takes over from splitting. The dream contents then reflect a both regressive and progressive temporality in the psychic processes, and this temporality can be worked through in its past (historical) and present (transference) dimensions. Conversely, whereas Guillaumin concentrates on the diachronic aspect of recapitulative dreams, I believe that the synchronic element is equally present and active.

Stewart: 'Ego-overwhelming dreams'

In a number of contributions, Stewart (1973, 1981 and 1992) describes a particular type of 'ego-overwhelming dreams', which, although experienced by the dreamer as threatening, in fact indicate progress in ego integration. They are similar in certain respects to dreams that turn over a page. Stewart distinguishes these 'ego-overwhelming dreams' from two other forms that he describes: 'ego-distancing dreams', which are defensive, and 'normal' dreams, which assume a symbolic meaning for the dreamer.

In this author's view, a progression paralleling the development of the transference can be discerned in the appearance of these various types of dreams during the psychoanalytic process. For instance, in 'ego-distancing dreams', which occur mainly at the beginning of the treatment, the dreamer sees himself as a passive spectator of the content of his own dreams and does not feel himself to be participating in them. Stewart considers these dreams to be based on a kind of projective identification in which the unwanted parts of the self are disavowed, split off and projected into objects that are placed at a distance – including the psychoanalyst. Later, as the patient gains an increased capacity for symbolization, 'ego-overwhelming dreams' appear; they commence once the patient recognizes that the analyst is a separate and different person, on whom he depends in order to progress. Stewart points out that these dreams are experienced by the dreamer as overwhelming because they reflect the patient's struggle to contain anxiety and to resist being overwhelmed by his drives, but this struggle may arise when the patient perceives the analyst as an object capable of tolerating ('holding', in Winnicott's sense) and containing (in Bion's sense) the anxieties generated by this potentially overwhelming situation. As to the third type, 'normal' dreams, these are correlated with the advanced phase of the analysis, in which the dreamer perceives the symbolic meaning of his dreams and feels actively involved in them, even if at times submerged and passive; they are then perceived by the dreamer as dreams and not as reality.

The same author (Stewart 1992) gives the example of a psychotic patient with an encapsulated transsexual delusion; he presents a number of this patient's 'ego-overwhelming dreams', which resemble the dreams I describe in some respects. For instance, Stewart notes that the changes he observes in the transference relationship were followed by dreams that reflect the prior intrapsychic change in the dreamer. In one case, after the analyst had noticed that his male patient was beginning to accept the idea that the fantasy of being a woman and the fantasy of being a man were inside himself (and not projected into another person), and after the patient had perceived the psychoanalyst as having the voice of his mother and the voice of his father, the patient had two simultaneous dreams. This frightened him, because he thought that having such 'split' dreams meant that he was about to go mad. Stewart points out, on the one hand, that the patient had this dream *after* realizing that he had a split inside himself, and, on the other, that the dream came after the patient had perceived the analyst as separate and different from himself.

In this paper the author particularly emphasizes that, in each episode, the changes in the dream experience were preceded by changes in the transference relationship:

[. . .] it is from the development of the external interpersonal relationships in the transference, where experiences of space, mobility, and separateness arise, that internalization of these processes and experiences occur to give rise to experiences of internal space, mobility, and separateness as manifested in these dream experiences. It is in the context of the constant interchange between these external and internal processes that growth and positive psychic change occur.

(Stewart 1992: 39)

In his theoretical discussion of the part played by the analyst in the emergence of these different kinds of dreams, Stewart takes up the concept of the dream screen introduced by Lewin (1946). On the one hand, he suggests that the dream screen represents not only the wish for fusion and the disavowal of hostility towards the breast, as shown by Rycroft (1951), but also the wish for a breast (mother) that can survive, contain and take care of the unwanted aspects of the self (p. 34). On the other hand, Stewart connects the idea of the dream screen with that of the dream space (Khan 1962), as well as with the concept of the dream container introduced by Segal (1973). For Segal, 'the psychic space of the dream ultimately derives from the breast containing projective identification, not a dream-screen in terms of Lewin but a dream container' (Segal 1973: 13). In Stewart's view,

the dream-screen represents a breast that is wished for but has never been adequately experienced as able to contain the projective identifications, whereas the dream container, from which she [Segal] postulates that psychic space is derived, represents the analyst who can contain the projective identifications, associated emotions, and anxieties.

(Stewart 1992: 35)

Stewart's observations on 'ego-overwhelming dreams' are similar to my own in a number of respects, such as the appearance of dreams with anxiety-inducing manifest content during phases of integration, and their occurrence after a change in the transference relationship. However, as to the timing of their emergence, this author places them in the context of the long-term trans-formations that take place during the treatment; in his opinion, 'ego-distancing dreams' precede 'ego-overwhelming dreams' before the latter assume their full symbolic value – whereas dreams that turn over a page can, in my opinion, occur at any time in the psychoanalytic process. Again, as he is interested mainly in the manifest content of such dreams, Stewart has taken little account of the close relationship between the latent content of dreams of this kind and the nature of the change that has just occurred – a correlation that is so impressive to the psychoanalyst. Finally, to judge from his clinical examples, the analyst seems to allow the patient to work through the anxiety resulting from an 'ego-overwhelming dream' himself, with a minimum of intervention on the analyst's part; this suggests that the patients in question have acquired sufficient capacity for symbolization to be able to cope with the experience of an ego-overwhelming dream and eventually to overcome it.

9

Classical and post-Freudian approaches

The classical approach, its developments and limits

The Interpretation of Dreams: Still the primary source today

Freud set forth his innovative ideas on dreams mainly in *The Interpretation of Dreams* (1900a), summarizing them in 'On dreams' (1901a). More than a century later, the work in which he presents his conception of dream life remains the most important and indeed obligatory source in the field of psychoanalysis that was his creation. Although post-Freudian psychoanalytic developments and subsequent progress in various scientific fields – in particular, the neurosciences – have broadened our knowledge of the mechanisms involved in dream formation, no new theory has superseded Freud's. And if one had, surely the psychoanalysts themselves would have been the first to realize it.

As we know, Freud's view is that dreams express the fulfilment of an unsatisfied unconscious wish, their formation resulting from a compromise whereby forbidden wishes can be fulfilled in the dream without the knowledge of the repression-inducing censorship. Dreams are triggered by an event of the previous day, around which a deeper-lying conflict stemming from unsatisfied wishes liable to disturb sleep is organized. Whereas the wish is hardly, if at all, disguised in children's dreams – little Anna dreamed of the strawberries she was denied on the previous day – the wish underlying adult dreams is generally no longer recognizable: because the satisfaction of these wishes might entail anxiety and guilt, they are repressed by the censorship. The *dream work* is responsible for the psychic activity of transforming unacceptable dream thoughts (the latent content) into thoughts that can be tolerated by the ego (the manifest content), so that dreams serve as the guardian of sleep. These transformations are effected by various mechanisms, which I shall briefly enumerate: condensation, displacement, reversal into the opposite, secondary revision, distortion, and considerations of representability.

At this point I should have liked to say more about Freud's conception of dreams for the benefit of readers whose curiosity I have surely aroused. By so doing, however, I should be running the risk not only of exceeding the bounds I have set myself in this book, but also of failing, in the attempt to summarize Freud's thought, to do justice to its richness and complexity. Whereas *The Interpretation of Dreams*, an opus teeming with ideas and examples of detailed dream analyses, constitutes an inexhaustible source of reflections and inspiration, it nevertheless remains an imposing work that is not easy to read. The brief paper 'On dreams' (1901a), in which Freud presents a clearly organized summary of his ideas, is thus an excellent introduction to it. Yet it is worth noting, as Anzieu (1988) points out, that the 'classical' style in which Freud presents his ideas in 'On dreams' contrasts starkly with the 'baroque' style that inspires *The Interpretation of Dreams* – a polarity that demonstrates how psychoanalytic writing constantly oscillates between didacticism and inspiration.

Freud was to stay faithful to his conception of dream theory as formulated in 1900, which, unlike other aspects of his theories, underwent only minor subsequent changes. However, the study of dreams remained an important concern for him throughout his life, as the notes he added to successive editions of *The Interpretation of Dreams* confirm (Grubrich-Simitis 2000). One of the main changes Freud made to his dream theory followed his description of the second topography, in which he introduced the notion of the superego in place of the dream 'censorship', from then on seeing the function of the dream as that of reconciling the demands of the id and of the superego (Freud 1933a [1932]). But although he presented new hypotheses from 1920 on, Freud did not develop the idea that the dream work has the aim not only of reconciling the forbidden wish with the superego or ego, but also – in accordance with today's view – of achieving a compromise in, or resolution of, the fundamental conflict between the life and death drives. We shall return to this point later, as the formation of dreams that turn over a page seems to involve a dream work directed towards finding a compromise not only between repressed conflicts but also, at a primitive level of mental functioning, in the fundamental conflict between the life and death drives.

As in the past, Freudian dream theory continues to inspire a very large number of publications in both the psychoanalytic and non-psychoanalytic fields. However, if, as I now wish to do, we attempt to identify psychoanalytic works that offer the reader an overall view of the subject, the choice proves to be limited. Sharpe's *Dream Analysis*, published in 1937, is an excellent introduction to the interpretation of dreams in the context of psychoanalytic treatment and is as relevant today as when it was written. Outstanding contributions from a variety of psychoanalytic orientations have been assembled in various recent compilations, such as *Essential Papers on Dreams* (Lansky 1992), *The Dream*

Discourse Today (Flanders 1993) and *Dreaming and Thinking* (Perelberg 2000). To find significant French-language contributions – apart from that of Guillaumin (1979) mentioned earlier and some isolated references in papers and a few books that will not be mentioned here – we have to go back to 1972 ('L'espace du rêve', *Nouvelle Revue Française de Psychanalyse*, No. 5) or even further (Fain & David 1963). Although the centenary of the publication of Freud's *Interpretation of Dreams* rekindled interest in dream analysis in 2000, Flanders (1993) points out that relatively few contributions on dreams have appeared in the last three or four decades. In this author's view, the reason is the growing importance assigned to transference analysis: 'the transference [. . .] has become the royal road to the understanding of the patient's emotional and mental life' (Flanders 1993: 13). Even so, dream analysis is found to have lost none of its value in clinical psychoanalysis, for most of the clinical examples presented in the current literature are illustrated by one of the patient's dreams.

An example of a wish-fulfilment dream: Tania

As an illustration of a dream that fulfils an unconscious wish, I have chosen one reported to me by Tania a few months after the page-turning dream examined in detail in Chapter 7. After that dream, I had noticed a change in the nature of her subsequent dreams. I attributed this to a better integration of her ego and of her object relations, and to her growing capacity to perceive their symbolic meaning and to link it to her experience of the transference, with a minimum of intervention on my part. As she gradually became more conscious of the symbolic transference meaning of hitherto repressed dream contents, Tania gained more and more insight into various aspects of her female identity, which she then became able to reconquer for herself.

At the beginning of one session, Tania brought me the following dream: 'A man was following me in the street; he seemed to want to seduce me, perhaps even to rape me. I was with a girlfriend, to whom I had entrusted my handbag, which contained my valuables as well as my identity papers, and she had hidden it so as not to attract the attention of thieves. I found myself bereft, with nothing that belonged to me. The dream ended there, but, oddly enough, it did not frighten me.' Tania told me that the dream reminded her of an episode of the previous day. While she was in a clothes shop with this girlfriend, a pleasant salesman had made a pass at her. She had at first thought that he was trying to chat up her friend, but then realized that his attentions were in fact directed to herself, Tania. Although initially offended, she acknowledged that she had felt a certain pleasure in having advances made to her and that she had even been turned on by this unknown man. She commented: 'In the dream, it is probably I who want to be seduced by him and not the other way round, because it is after all my dream.' I was surprised by the accuracy of her interpretation of the reversal performed by the dream work, which meant that Tania was in the process of re-owning a sexual desire which she had for a long time defended against. My own view was that Tania had long got rid of her own desires by projective identification, with the result that she did not really feel herself to be a woman; this was because she had unconsciously deposited her own desires (for example, her handbag) and the anxieties associated with her envy and aggression either in men whom she experienced as dangerous seducers or in women in her circle whom she felt to be attractive to men, whereas she did not see herself as attractive. In my opinion, it was this aspect of the defensive process that appeared in this dream.

Tania continued the course of her associations: 'Yesterday I visited another girlfriend and admired how she had applied a feminine touch to her interior. I felt quite jealous when I thought of the pleasant relationship a woman like her must have with her husband.'

Myself: 'Doesn't this dream suggest that you would like to rediscover the feeling of becoming an attractive woman? And do you not want to get into a relationship with a man like the one that your friend, who seems so much at ease with her femininity, has with her husband?'

Tania: 'At first I always felt that men – including my father – had nothing but bad intentions towards me, and I felt myself to be a victim whose only defence was to run away from them contemptuously. Now I can accept having desires, even for an unknown man like the one who made a pass at me yesterday, and I feel that my feminine side is awakening. Even so, I defend myself against it in the dream: is that why I entrusted my handbag to my friend? Isn't the hand-bag the symbol of my female sexuality?' Tania remained silent for a moment, and then added that she could see yet another displacement in this dream, which had to do with me: 'I was just thinking that the man in the dream who is after me must surely be you. If so, does the dream mean that I want to join with you in crossing a forbidden sexual boundary I am ashamed to talk to you about, because I feel it as a guilty attack on you?' The session ended at this point.

The latent content of this dream reveals Tania's unconscious wish to seduce, whereas, by virtue of the guilt feelings that deprive her of her heterosexual desires and female organs, the manifest content expresses the compromise achieved by the dream, displacing the responsibility for the desire on to the man who is trying to seduce her and her femininity on to the girlfriend to whom Tania entrusted her bag, the symbol of her female identity. The dream also illustrates the idea that the dreamer's ego must have attained sufficient cohesion and integration for mechanisms such as repression or displacement to operate within a whole ego. During this session, we thus find that Tania's thought navigates easily between the different parts of her psychic world, which form a whole: she herself explores the content of her dream through her associations, which are made up not only of residues of the previous day but also of thoughts that spontaneously occur to her with the progress of her reflecting. Again, the symbolic sense, which was for a long time partly lacking in her, enables her to link the manifest and latent contents, as for example when she becomes aware of different meaning levels condensed in the image of the woman's handbag containing her 'valuables' and 'identity papers'. This 'navigation' in an internal world that is no longer fragmented as it was before enables Tania to end the session by spontaneously relating the meaning of this dream to the transference relationship, in a direct oedipal context that she puts into words.

Of course, even if Tania shows such great insight in this example, not every patient will necessarily discover the latent meaning of a wish-fulfilment dream for himself. In most cases, a patient who has a dream with classical structure does not spontaneously perceive its symbolic meaning, but discovers it only with the psychoanalyst's help. Again, a session of this kind is a rare privilege, and does not mean that others will regularly offer the same quality of insight. As the subsequent sessions of Tania's analysis showed, psychoanalytic work proceeds by alternate steps forward and back, and development takes place more in accordance with a spiral pattern than in a linear manner.

Post-Freudian contributions to dream theory

Beyond classical theory

Clearly, then, whereas many dreams can be explained and analysed on the basis of the classical theory, that theory does not by itself suffice to analyse or explain the formation of all dreams, and, in particular, that of dreams that turn over a page and their characteristics. For this purpose I have found it essential to invoke the concepts of unconscious fantasy, projective identification and oscillation between the paranoid-schizoid and depressive positions. These notions were introduced with the psychoanalytic conceptions of Klein and the post-Kleinians, with a view to understanding the transformations underlying the formation of such dreams in terms of the transference relationship, ego structure and the processes of symbolization. However, although primitive defences are involved in the formation of the dreams I describe, this does not necessarily mean that these dreams occur only in psychotic patients or borderlines, for I have observed them in patients of all kinds, including those whose psychic organization is predominantly neurotic.

In my view, the classical and contemporary theories are by no means mutually exclusive but instead complement each other. After all, the classical theory is based on the postulate that the ego is capable of appropriately repressing and of performing the dream work, the dreamer's capacity to symbolize being taken for granted. However, as the last example shows, in order for repression to operate, it is essential for the dreamer's ego to have attained a sufficient degree of cohesion and unity for repression to take over from splitting.

What is integration?

Klein's overall view is that the mind is never totally integrated, integration being one of the main tasks of development. She considers that what stimulates the process of integration is the pressure of anxiety, which impels the mind towards a higher level of maturity, together with the forward thrust resulting from biological development.

At different stages in her career, Klein saw the task of integration in different ways. She began by drawing attention to the struggle to integrate the internal parental imagos into a mature superego. Then, between 1932 and 1946, she introduced the notions of the depressive position and the paranoid–schizoid position, which involve the integration of good and bad objects during the course of development, as splitting becomes increasingly realistic. Finally, with the introduction of the concept of projective identification in 1946, she set about demonstrating the mechanisms involved in the integration of the self itself (Hinshelwood 1989).

In clinical practice, Kleinian technique has placed more and more emphasis on the integration of split-off elements within the self. An essential aspect of the psychoanalyst's work is therefore to identify the scattered elements of the transference relationship that have been split off and deposited by projective identification in different objects of the patient's external and internal reality, with a view to putting them back together by interpretation and to facilitating better integration of the patient's psychic and relational life.

Note that several different types of splits and splitting are possible, which the English language can distinguish more subtly than French – for example, splitting up (*morcellement*), splitting off (*détachement par clivage*), separating off (*séparation par clivage*), or the fragmenting split (*clivage par fragmentation*) (Hinshelwood 2000: 3). In his preface to the French edition of *A Dictionary of Kleinian Thought*, Hinshelwood points out that this rich vocabulary was surely very advantageous to Klein in her development of the fundamental concept of splitting; he adds: 'I wonder whether the limitations of the French language associated with this fundamental concept [splitting] might have the effect of making Melanie Klein's thought appear less subtle to the French-speaking reader, who may thus be inclined to take less interest in her ideas' (ibid.).

The elaborative function in dreams

Finally, in keeping with my contention that the elaborative function plays a central part in the formation of dreams that turn over a page, I should like to point out that many contemporary psychoanalysts assign more importance to this function than Freud did. For instance, Grinberg (1967) distinguished dreams by their function and, specifically, defined 'elaborative dreams' as belonging to the depressive position and containing reparative wishes. In the view of Meltzer (1984), dreams seek to create a symbolic form allowing the emotional experience to be represented and contributing to the solution of problems. Segal (1991) places particular emphasis on the role of the dream work in the search for a fantasy solution to conflicts at different levels. She notes, too, that, whereas Freud developed the concept of working through, he did not apply it explicitly to the dream work seen as one of the ways of elaborating a conflict. In her opinion, what is lacking in psychosis is precisely the psychic work of conflict elaboration, which resembles the process of working through that takes place in dreams.

Dream-work-α

The elaborative function of dreams occupies an important position in Bion's conception, which differs radically from that of Freud and the post-Freudians while at the same time complementing it. In *Cogitations*, Bion (1992) portrays dreams as the result of a failure of the function of dream-work-α, rather than as attempts to resolve unconscious conflicts in accordance with the view generally accepted today. The following summary of his conception introduces a different point of view into the understanding of certain aspects of the formation of dreams that turn over a page.

Bion's chosen starting point is Freud's notion of the dream work, which he expands by introducing the idea of the 'dream-work-α' as something that operates continuously night and day, and not just at night. Dream-work-α is applied to both internal sensory impressions and the stimuli originating from the facts of external reality. The experiences concerned are within the area of consciousness but are not accessible to memory as long as they have not been 'dreamed' – that is, transformed by the α function. The object of the dream-work-α is therefore to transform impressions in the crude state by making them pre-communicable – a transformation that constitutes what Bion calls the 'domain of the dream'. This is defined as a storehouse in which impressions are preserved in the form of an amorphous mass of disconnected and un-differentiated elements that may be experienced as bad and dangerous, or alternatively as good, according to personality-related factors.

On the basis of these premises, Bion considers that the dream-work-α can be utilized in two main ways: first, transformation of internal and external stimuli so that they can be stored and subsequently recalled and synthesized; and, second, use of the dream images to expel unwanted emotional experiences.

Where the dream-work-α operates satisfactorily, these elements may assume different forms – for example, visual, auditory or olfactory – which are then incorporated in a pictorial symbol. The proper functioning of this process is the prerequisite for the capacity to transform conscious material into unconscious material appropriate to 'unconscious waking thought'. Bion likens it to a process of digestion: 'In this respect the dream seems to play a part in the mental life of the individual which is analogous to the digestive processes in the alimentary life of the individual' (Bion 1992: 45). This conception then enables him to define the dream – as 'ordinarily reported' – as a sign of indigestion, or, more precisely, as 'a symptom of mental indigestion' reflecting a 'failure of dream-work-α' (ibid.: 68). He attributes this failure to various causes, chief among which is the fact that the visual impression is placed in the service of excessive projective identification in order to rid the psyche of the unwanted parts of emotional experience: in this case the 'dream itself is [. . .] felt to be an act of evacuation in much the same way as the visual hallucination is felt to be a positive act of expulsion through the eyes' (ibid.: 67). This failure may extend as far as the collapse of the capacity to dream; and Bion considers that one of the main causes of this breakdown of the synthesizing function of dream-work-α is the role played by the superego – a conflict to which we shall return in the next chapter when we discuss the relations between the negative therapeutic reaction and the capacity to work through a dream.

An examination of dreams that turn over a page in the light of Bion's ideas suggests that such dreams result partly from a failure of dream-work-α and partly from a successful process of working through.

10

Formation of dreams that turn over a page: Hypotheses

The wish for integration and its expression in dreams

The ego as an entity subject to constant recasting

I should now like to present an overall view of the hypotheses that seem to me to account best for the main characteristics of dreams that turn over a page as described and illustrated with clinical examples in this book. They are all based on the idea that such dreams arise during phases of integration in the context of the constant processes of recasting undergone by the ego – transformations that can be understood as oscillations between the paranoid-schizoid and depressive positions.

My clinical experience has gradually led me to conclude that *these dreams originate within the incessant state of flux characterizing an ego that by no means constitutes a static organization but results from a dynamic equilibrium subject to constant recasting – an equilibrium that is never achieved once and for all.* Unlike 'classical' dreams, which are observed in patients whose ego possesses sufficient cohesion and unity, I believe that *dreams that turn over a page are a function of the incessant back-and-forth movements whereby the parts of the self alternately become scattered and put themselves together again.* These constant successive swings between frag-mentation and integration can be conceptualized as oscillations between the paranoid-schizoid and depressive positions, for which Bion used the notation PS ↔ D. If mental functioning is conceived in these terms, it is understandable that symptoms, fantasies or dreams with primitive content, as well as destructive drives, may arise not only at the time of termination of analysis, when integration-related phenomena are particularly active, but also at any period in the psychoanalytic process.

The oscillations between the paranoid-schizoid and depressive positions impact not only on the structure of subject–object relations but also on the function of dreams, which thus varies according to the predominant type of psychic functioning. For instance, when the ego tends towards integration, mechanisms associated with repression become established, whereas, when primitive defences gain the upper hand, the very function of the dream may be altered, as in psychotic or borderline patients in particular (Segal 1991). In these conditions of ego dysfunction, the dream's function is no longer that of working through and symbolization, but of getting rid of intolerable contents by depositing them in the psychoanalyst's mind, so that the dream contents are enacted in the session instead of fully playing their part as communications between patient and analyst.

Coexistence of primitive and neurotic defences

Inherent in my conception of the psychical apparatus here is the notion that primitive defence mechanisms coexist in every individual alongside more mature defence mechanisms, in variable proportions. This view is based on the idea of splitting of the ego, which Freud first defined as a mechanism characteristic of psychosis but which he later postulated as existing also in neurosis: 'The view which postulates that in all psychoses there is a *splitting of the ego* could not call for so much notice if it did not turn out to apply to other states more like the neuroses and, finally, to the neuroses themselves' (Freud 1940a [1938]: 202).

Bion (1962) was subsequently to use this proposition as the basis for distinguishing between the psychotic and non-psychotic parts of the personality – a conception that occupies a central position in our present-day view of psychic functioning. After all, if we accept that there is a difference between psychotic and non-psychotic ego functioning within each individual's psyche, and that primitive and mature defences coexist in variable proportions, it becomes clear that dreams that turn over a page can arise in any patient. For the same reasons, we can also understand how such dreams *may appear at any point in the psychoanalytic process,* as we have seen, and not only in connection with the approach of termination.

Again, although primitive defence mechanisms were first detected in psychosis, this does not of course mean that such dreams occur mainly in patients whose personality organization is predominantly psychotic or borderline. I personally *have encountered dreams of this type in analysands with a wide variety of psychic organizations, ranging from predominantly neurotic to predominantly psychotic structures.* However, on closer reflection, in particular in the light of the observations of Arieti (1963) and Blechner (2000), I noticed that *dreams that turn over a page do indeed appear to be more frequent in patients in whom primitive defences are more developed than neurotic defences.*

78

The 'return' of split-off parts of the self

It was the frequently observed coincidence between a dream with regressive content and a phase of progress in the concomitant processes of psychic integration that led me to reflect on the nature of a – from the viewpoint of classical dream theory – seeming contradiction. *I suggested that, in order for such a dream to arise during a phase of integration, the ego must at the time be confronted with the return of unwanted projections hitherto disavowed, split off and expelled by projective identification into internal or external objects* (J.-M. Quinodoz 1999). As stated in Chapter 2, I wish to emphasize that I am here using the word 'return' in the sense of a re-owning by the ego of previously expelled parts, and not of a 'return of the disavowed' analogous to the 'return of the repressed' – that is, the reappearance in the form of symptoms of what had been repressed.

The sense of 'buoyancy' and psychic integration

This return of split-off parts of the self, occurring at a time when they are better accepted by the ego, is made possible by the transformations taking place in the transference relationship: in working through the depressive position, the patient is better able to distinguish between subject and object, and his ego can thus attain a higher degree of cohesion. During the course of this process of integration, persecutory anxieties, splitting and omnipotence diminish, so that the withdrawal of projections gives rise to the return of parts of the self as introjection is reinforced. These parts may then be deemed to belong to the self, thus providing the dreamer with a sense of internal cohesion and unity in his rediscovered personality.

To describe the sense of internal cohesion experienced by a patient in the working through of separation and object-loss anxieties within the analysand–analyst relationship, I previously introduced the concept of 'buoyancy':

> For me, *the sense of identity stemming from integration and the accompanying sense of buoyancy result from the gathering together of the essential aspects of the ego and their continuous re-organization in a unified ego, or rather an ego in constant search of unification.*
>
> (J.-M. Quinodoz 1991: 185, italics in the original)

Similarly, an equilibrium within the ego may be seen to arise in the psychoanalytic process when the analysand rediscovers crucial aspects of himself, so to speak taking them with him and making them his own, while at the same time becoming capable of detaching himself from important aspects of himself that nevertheless remain tied to objects, which must be given up:

> At one and the same time, therefore, there is a *recovery* of essential aspects of the ego which had previously been 'lost', in particular by splitting and

projection (on to external objects, internal objects or parts of the body seen as objects), a constant *re-organization* of these re-discovered aspects of the ego in a unified ego, and a preparedness to *forgo* taking everything with one.

(ibid.: 185–6)

A threat to the cohesion of the dreamer's ego

However, the reintegration of what had been projected not only gives rise to a sense of relief and cohesion in the dreamer but also triggers renewed anxiety, because the ego is momentarily confronted with the fear of confusion and madness. That is why the dreamer often exclaims 'I have had a crazy dream!' or 'I am afraid of going mad again!' and tends to appeal to the analyst for help in working through.

The anxiety thus expressed by the dreamer can be explained in various ways; some of its components emerged in our examination of the characteristics of these dreams in Chapter 2. As stated, if we consider Freud's successive theories of anxiety, first (1919h) comes the notion of the uncanny, a composite feeling resulting from the juxtaposition of the familiar and the unknown. This is followed by his second theory of anxiety (1926d [1925]), which attributes the phenomenon to the sense of helplessness (*Hilflosigkeit*) experienced by an individual when confronted with the threat of separation and object loss; anxiety here functions as an alarm signal. Finally, Freud adduces the part played by splitting of the ego and its structural consequences (1940a [1938]).

Hence one of the main sources of anxiety in a dreamer confronted with a dream that turns over a page is *the critical moment when the dreamer retrospectively becomes conscious of the anxiety-generating effects of the splitting phenomena which had affected his ego.* This onset of consciousness coincides with the moment when the ego regains its unity and cohesion. In other words, it is only when the patient comes to experience the effects of disavowal, splitting, idealization and projective identification that he feels the effects of an ego fragmentation that had hitherto remained unconscious. The dreamer's anxiety thus stems from a sense that the ego is threatened by the split rather than from the recurrence of repressed contents – in accordance with Freud's 'third' theory of anxiety, according to which the ego 'makes use of the sensations of anxiety as a signal to give a warning of dangers that threaten its integrity' (1940a [1938]: 199).

From another point of view, this moment of integration may also be deemed to correspond to the working through of the depressive position as described by Klein, who points out that it is only when the object comes to be perceived as whole that the situation of object loss can become established: 'Not until the object is loved *as a whole* can its loss be felt as a whole' (Klein 1934: 264, italics in the original). This might perhaps justify the parallel hypothesis that it is when the self is perceived and loved as a whole that its loss can be experienced as a whole loss and true mourning can take place.

The gathering together of the parts of the self as expressed in dreams

Whereas the manifestations of projection of split-off parts of the self are more familiar and relatively easy to observe clinically, the opposite process, that of the gathering together and owning by the ego of previously split-off and projected parts, seems to me to be less well known and to have been studied less. Yet this phenomenon of integration of the scattered parts of the self can sometimes be discerned in the contents of certain dreams, which portray it in particularly expressive and graphic form.

This is illustrated in my book on the effects of working through separation and object-loss anxieties on the psychoanalytic process, in which I pointed out that the gathering together of the scattered parts of the self that takes place in the course of the working through of mourning in the transference relationship is sometimes expressed in the content of certain dreams (J.-M. Quinodoz 1991). The dreamer here most often represents himself as having to catch a train or plane and to sort his luggage into the essential items to be taken with him and those he is prepared to leave behind. The train or plane is, in my view, a symbolic representation of an ego that has become capable of containing (i.e., a container) through identification with the containing capacity of the psychoanalyst, whereas the luggage represents the scattered parts of the self (i.e., contents) undergoing the characteristic sorting of mourning work in progress: some items are abandoned, while others, considered essential, are taken with the subject. This process of integration often gives rise to an affect I have called the sense of buoyancy, which the patient sometimes expresses by telling the analyst that he feels he has succeeded in 'flying with his own wings'. I added that such dreams afford valuable information about hidden aspects of the ego that have remained unconsciously attached to objects and difficult to detect, thus standing in the way of the sense of integration and buoyancy.

This process of gathering together and integrating different split-off parts of the self is clearly represented in a dream mentioned by Segal (1991). In it, a female analysand puts together the pieces of a jigsaw puzzle, thereby reconstituting a house that represents her complete family. The author shows in her commentary that, among the changes accompanying the depressive position, the withdrawal of projective identification gives rise to a change in the nature of fantasy, from a part-object relationship to a whole-object situation such as the parental couple, as repression gradually takes over from the more primitive defences of splitting, idealization and projection. This dream of putting together the pieces of the jigsaw thus represented the mental activity necessary for restoring the patient's psyche, which is experienced from then on as a united family.

81

A dream that illustrates the sorting of the scattered parts of the self

The following short example of one of my patients in the process of terminating illustrates how certain dreams use symbolic images to express the sorting that precedes a separation. This dream came some time after we had agreed to fix a date for the end of the analysis – a decision taken on the patient's own initiative, which I approved because the work concerned had brought about major changes in his life. The dream was as follows: 'I dreamed that I was leaving home to travel to distant parts. I was going to take with me only what was necessary and leave the rest behind. Oddly enough, though, it was not I who did the sorting, but my neighbour, whom I had called in to help. For example, he himself decided which of my books were going to stay behind and which he was to pack up in the cases. In the dream, I was pleased; I looked at him and was happy not to have to do this painful job myself. But when I woke up, I was very annoyed!'

The patient spontaneously understood that this dream was connected with our forthcoming separation; however, he was surprised to dream of handing over the responsibility for choosing his luggage to someone else: 'I can't understand why I should dream that my neighbour – presumably you – was entrusted with something that concerns only me. I thought I had taken responsibility for my decision to leave you: does this dream mean that I don't really feel involved?' The patient ended the session with an association to the memory of the frequent moves he had experienced in his childhood, when he had seen his parents pack their children's cases, although they had in fact asked what they wanted to take with them.

I believe that this dream showed first of all the sorting which, in my view, represented the mourning process undertaken by the patient as the termination approached, putting together the essential parts of his psychoanalytic experience that he was going to take with him. Then came the novel aspects of his need for passive dependence in relation to the figure of the neighbour who represented me. There is no doubt that, at the very moment when this patient was becoming capable of taking the initiative to terminate his analysis, the approach of the termination had flushed out unconscious fantasies associated with his passive tendencies that had hitherto remained concealed, in the sense of a dream that turns over a page.

Dreams as an expression of the conflict between the life and death drives

Searching for a resolution of the fundamental conflict

According to our present-day conception, the dream work involves achieving not only a compromise that will reconcile the forbidden wish with the superego and the ego, as the classical theory postulates, but also a compromise in the fundamental conflict between the life and death drives. This contemporary view highlights the central part played by the dream work both in working through unconscious conflicts by repression and the symbolic function as achievements of an ego that has acquired sufficient cohesion, and in finding a resolution of more primitive conflicts affecting the cohesion of the ego itself.

For in view of the part played by primitive defences such as disavowal, splitting, idealization, projection and projective identification, the ego may be deemed subject to contradictory and conflicting tendencies that affect its very structure: when anxiety is too intense, the ego tends to split and project, and hence to fragment; conversely, when anxiety declines, so too do splitting and projection, which give way to introjection. These dynamic changes that constantly modify the structure of the ego may be seen as reflecting the constant oscillations between the paranoid-schizoid and depressive positions – oscillations that themselves mirror the fundamental conflict between the life drive, in which the tendency towards integration predominates, and the death drive, in which fragmentation holds sway. When the integrative tendency becomes established, the split between ideal and persecutory objects is diminished and projection declines, gradually giving way to a trend towards self and object integration; in my view, dreams that turn over a page arise in the aftermath of this psychic work.

Fulfilment of an unconscious wish for integration?

On this basis, we may postulate that *the gathering together of the scattered parts of the self observed in dreams that turn over a page might form part of the search for a resolution of the structural conflict between a tendency of the ego towards integration and a tendency towards psychic fragmentation, influenced by the conflict between the life and death drives.*

Perhaps we can go further and hypothesize that, just as a dream, according to the classical theory, represents a compromise for the fulfilment of a repressed wish, so too the gathering together of the scattered parts of the self constitutes a compromise for the fulfilment of a wish – the wish for cohesion and unity of the ego. If so, might the compromise achieved be between a tendency to integration and a tendency to fragmentation within the conflict between the life and death drives, with the life drive as the engine of integration? *In this way, might the dreams I describe also conform to the fundamental mechanism of dream formation postulated by the classical theory, while at the same time, on another level, reflecting the fulfilment of a wish – a wish for integration that is never fully satisfied?*

The negative therapeutic reaction and dreams that turn over a page

Dreams and the negative therapeutic reaction

The hypothesis that one element of the dream work is the finding of a compromise in the conflict between the life and death drives naturally leads us to undertake a more detailed consideration of the relations between dreams that turn over a page and the negative therapeutic reaction. I first raised this subject in Chapter 4 and I shall return to it now, in particular in the light of the relevant work of Rosenfeld and O'Shaughnessy, as well as of the notion of the failure of dream-work-α, which Bion also places at the heart of a conflict between integration and retreat in the fact of psychic integration.

Overcoming and dreaming of a negative therapeutic reaction

Whether or not a negative therapeutic reaction can be overcome depends on a large number of factors on the part of both patient and psychoanalyst. Rosenfeld (1987) gives two examples. In the first, he shows that, as the patient concerned came to trust him more, he immediately felt inferior and almost smashed to pieces, so that he complained: 'What is the good of making any progress if I am torn to shreds afterwards?' (p. 89). The patient in Rosenfeld's second example overcomes a negative therapeutic reaction and subsequently brings two dreams having the characteristics of dreams that turn over a page.

This patient, Michael, had succeeded in overcoming a negative therapeutic reaction that had followed an important step forward in his emotional life. Immediately after this reaction, he dreamed that he had not only a penis but also a vagina; Rosenfeld tells us that the content of this dream later contributed significantly to resolving the conflict with his father and the transference situation. He adds that the dream could have been taken as regressive and interpreted as such – expressing, for example, the patient's unconscious wish for omnipotent possession of both sexes – but Rosenfeld interpreted it positively, in the sense of the patient's newly acquired capacity for representation of his feminine part in the context of psychic bisexuality. Then followed a second dream, accompanied by considerable anxiety, in which the analyst was represented by a woman; this too was interpreted positively by Rosenfeld: 'In spite of Michael's feeling of despair and fear of having spoilt everything the dream emphasized not the negative reaction but the positive progress which he felt he had made' (ibid.: 95). He adds, however, that these negative therapeutic reactions, which on the one hand serve to shock and on the other help the patient make progress, are relatively rare.

The clinical example of Michael thus shows that the capacity to overcome a negative therapeutic reaction is conditional upon the patient's having worked through the depressive position and become sufficiently capable of symbolization to represent primitive aspects of himself and to tolerate anxiety, as in a dream that succeeds in turning over a page. Again, Michael's two dreams – both the one in which he imagines having not only a penis but also a vagina, and that in which he represents the analyst as a woman – have points of similarity with the dreams I describe; they indicate better integration of the dreamer's psychic bisexuality. Finally, Rosenfeld explicitly points out that he interpreted not negatively, as he was tempted to do, but constructively – an aspect of technique that I have also stressed in connection with dreams that turn over a page.

A dream that fails in its elaborative function

I recently had occasion to discuss a contribution by O'Shaughnessy (2000) entitled 'Dreaming and not dreaming'. In this paper, the analyst considers the possible relations between a dream brought by one of her female patients and a dream that turns over a page as described by me. In the dream the patient was in a palace together with the Queen; the dream's content suddenly threw a very clear light on unconscious fantasies that had never hitherto appeared in the clinical material:

> Until her dream of the Queen's palace with its antiques and pictures revealed these image dreams to be pictures which are part of a wider underlying defensive phantasy, I had not even arrived at so clear a description of their nature as I have just given.
>
> (O'Shaughnessy 2000: 31)

In the first part of the session in which she brought this dream, the patient appeared to gain insight, but in the second part she turned in on herself; the analyst interpreted this as an enactment of the dream in the session, whereby the patient shut herself up in a fusion with the analyst in a similar way to the dream situation in which she had shut herself up in the palace with the Queen. The appearance of a lump in the patient's breast a few days before the dream seems to have contributed to the onset of an anxiety state accompanied by a hostile transference.

I commented that this patient's dream did indeed in some respects resemble a dream that turns over a page, in that it began by clearly presenting unconscious fantasies that revealed retrospectively what had been happening in the transference. However, it seems to me that this dream differed from those I describe because it eventually failed in its integrative function owing to the excess of anxiety that had resulted in its enactment in the second part of the session (J.-M. Quinodoz 2000d).

The destructive superego and the failure of dream-work-α

As discussed in the previous chapter, Bion considers that the dream-work-α – which operates continuously night *and* day – is the linchpin of the patient's capacity to transform psychic experiences. If this function is deficient, the patient feels that he is not dreaming or that he is incapable of 'dreaming' – in the widened sense of the term – because he is unable to synthesize the α elements; a conflict then arises between destructive and reparative tendencies.

To overcome such a deficiency, the patient must succeed in restoring the dream-work-α destroyed by splitting and projective identification, and in putting the scattered fragments of experience – whether α or β elements – back together. A number of factors may block this process of restoration – for example, hatred of reality or the threat of depression, but in particular the fear of the superego. This fear stems in turn from the fear that the process of restoration of fragments of visual images will inevitably entail the restoration of an extremely destructive superego. When the analyst attempts to identify the fragments the patient is seeking to juxtapose, 'the destructive super-ego emerges, and contemporaneous destructive attempts are made, at the instigation of the super-ego, to undo the attempts at juxtaposition and repair' (Bion 1992: 97). Bion stresses that the destructive attempts tend to occur outside rather than inside the sessions, whereas the patient succeeds in making his attempts at reparation within the sessions, because it is only there that he trusts in the external aid afforded him by the analyst's presence.

The clinical examples of Rosenfeld and O'Shaughnessy, like Bion's hypotheses, show that a patient's capacity to work through a dream depends on a number of factors, of which the most important are connected with his capacity to overcome the ambivalence arising out of his transference affects. A love/hate ambivalence is observed in the patient, whose ability to overcome it varies. Whereas it may in some cases allow the dreamer to 'turn over a page', in others it may prove impossible to overcome, possibly even leading to a negative therapeutic reaction, as a direct expression of the fundamental conflict in which the death drive gains the upper hand over the life drive. However, as Capozzi and De Masi (2001) point out, when the analyst is confronted by the anxiety accompanying a dream – whether it be a psychotic dream or a dream of the type that turns over a page – it is not easy to distinguish between the result of a difficulty in accepting integration and the manifestation of a psychotic part of the personality that terrifies the patient.

11

Impact: Clinical and aesthetic

Clinical impact of dreams that turn over a page

Relations between clinical and aesthetic impact

I should now like to flesh out the hypotheses outlined in the previous chapters by presenting some reflections on the impact of these dreams. I shall consider first the reasons why some dreams have a more powerful impact than others on both patient and analyst, especially in phases of integration, when the gathering together of the parts of the self is accompanied by a highly significant dream. I shall then attempt to draw a parallel between the clinical impact of such a dream and the aesthetic impact of a work of art, given the observed similarities between the two phenomena.

Intense evocative power

It is a matter of daily experience that our interest and curiosity as psychoanalysts are aroused whenever an analysand brings us a dream, because we expect it to help enlighten us about the problems currently exercising the patient. However, the degree of interest varies considerably from one dream to another, as well as with the dreamer's personality and with our countertransference. While some dreams make a stronger impression on us as psychoanalysts, others barely inspire us, or even leave us completely cold. This evocative power depends on a number of factors. It varies according to the phase of the treatment and with the patient's capacity, or incapacity, to report his dreams. It varies, too, with the abundance of the patient's dream representations and the relative breadth with which they unfold: as we have seen, the content of a dream can inform us not only about repressed conflicts but also about the many different organizational levels of the dreamer's drives, defences and personality structure. The wider the range of dream representations, the more likely it is that the dream will impress the psychoanalyst and stimulate his capacity to forge links within an increasingly multidimensional network.

For instance, if Tania's dream had a greater impact on me than her usual ones, this was because its evocative potential proved to be unexpectedly rich. On the one hand, its content presented her repressed conflicts as if on a stage – conflicts such as the emergence of heterosexual desires towards the unknown man, on the level of oedipal neurotic conflict. On the other, the dream revealed a complex gamut of primitive conflicts and defences, such as the awakening of Tania's destructive envy of her mother and, also, of her parental couple as represented by me. Other components were the recurrence of her ambivalence and of her latent homosexual tendencies in relation to persecutory anxieties. In a word, this dream afforded an overall view of her progress and her defences against it.

How is this clinical impact to be explained? The main factor was surely my surprise at suddenly discovering an extraordinarily coherent depiction, directed towards me, of the various facets of Tania's pathology in relation to her personality and the nature of her transference relationship. Then there was the impression of obviousness conveyed by the precision with which the dream content illustrated – virtually point by point and with marvellous imagery – the most complex psychic and relational mechanisms. This grand fresco provided me with a basis for delving more deeply into all aspects of the transference, and paved the way for subsequent interpretations.

Impact of the repressed, the disavowed and the split-off

In addition to the factors just mentioned, I believe that the clinical impact of certain dreams results from the ego's owning of hitherto disavowed and projected psychic fragments, which have come to be better accepted. In my view, in the phases of recasting and integration to which such dreams belong, the return of the disavowed and split-off parts endows the ego with a new-found cohesion, so that the mechanism of repression can begin working alongside splitting, and can eventually overlap with and supersede it. I would liken this phenomenon of the gathering together of the scattered parts of the ego during integration to the joining up of the pieces of a jigsaw puzzle – although this metaphor does not do full justice to the integrative process, which goes beyond the mere juxta-position of separate fragments. It is this effect that gives rise, in dreamer and analyst alike, to a sense of discovering something that has never before been seen, yet was already known.

At this point the question arises whether it is possible to distinguish clinically between dream representations connected with repression and those assignable to splitting. Splitting-related manifestations may be easier to identify when on a massive scale, for example in the case of a traumatic situation arising in a dream, especially if this is its first appearance. However, where the splits are less clear-cut and the situation more subtle, it will be harder to distinguish between split-off and repressed contents on both the metapsychological and clinical levels.

Clinical impact and preliminary interviews

With regard to the effect of a dream on the psychoanalyst, it seems to me that a parallel can be drawn between the evocative power of a dream that turns over a page and that occasioned by a patient's material *during the initial interviews* when he first requests the help of an analyst. It is a matter of common experience for an analyst that the situation of a first meeting makes a very powerful impression owing to the patient's spontaneous tendency to present the essentials of his unconscious problem situation during this first contact. *These projective phenomena are connected with the patient's unconscious wish to find, in the person of the analyst, a psychic container offering a potential resolution of his conflicts.* The content of these projections then constitutes a grand fresco that sums up the patient's unconscious problem situation and personality structure. The analyst will use this clinical material as a basis for evaluating the possibility, or otherwise, of embarking on psychoanalytic work. Brief as it is, this opening on to the unconscious is wide-ranging and meaningful enough to afford the analyst an outline of the future work 'programme', which will extend over a number of years.

Moreover, a similar search for a psychic container may be observed *at the beginning of each session*, albeit on a smaller scale, as the patient's first words often comprise a condensed version of the material to be developed during the session.

Such phenomena of projective identification are also seen, although in more pronounced form, in patients with more primitive than neurotic defences. That is why the unconscious of psychotic and borderline patients is more accessible to an observer. According to Bion (1992: 71), this transparency is due to these patients' difficulty in 'digesting' their psychic experiences owing to a 'lack of capacity for α', with the result that these 'elements remain detectable because the patient cannot make them unconscious'.

As regards the clinical impact of unconscious productions on the analyst's mind, then, parallels may be drawn between the phenomena occurring in the initial interviews and at the beginning of sessions, on the one hand, and those observed when certain dreams burst on to the scene, on the other.

Aesthetic impact of dreams that turn over a page

Do works of art and dreams have a similar impact?

In reflecting on the powerful impression made by certain dreams, such as dreams that turn over a page, I wondered whether a parallel could be drawn between the impact of these dreams and the aesthetic impact of a work of art on the spectator.

In my view, there are indeed many similarities between the mental impact of a dream on a psychoanalyst and that produced by works of art, for these too mirror the artist's unconscious problem situation, which he seeks to resolve by way of an artistic form whose effect on the spectator may be more or less intense. My ideas are based mainly on Segal's contributions (1952, 1957, 1991) on the role of symbolism and unconscious fantasy in dreams and art.

Aesthetic pleasure: Freud's view

Let me begin with a brief recapitulation of Freud's ideas on the subject. The discoveries of psychoanalysis – in particular, that of unconscious fantasy and symbolism – had enabled him to understand works of art on a new and deeper level as symbolic expressions. In his opinion, what makes a work of art ring artistically true is the artist's intuitive knowledge of universal fantasies. Freud's views on the application of psychoanalysis to art and literature are essentially based on the mechanism of repression. The wishes expressed in art works are repressed wishes, unacceptable to the conscious mind and partially disguised, so that our pleasure stems from our being induced to accept these hidden thoughts insidiously. Freud holds that the impact of a work of art results primarily from the intention and emotion the artist seeks to communicate to us:

> In my opinion, what grips us so powerfully can only be the artist's *intention*, in so far as he has succeeded in expressing it in his work and in getting us to understand it. I realize that this cannot be merely a matter of *intellectual* comprehension; what he aims at is to awaken in us the same emotional attitude, the same mental constellation as that which in him produced the impetus to create.
>
> (Freud 1914b: 212)

However, as Segal points out, Freud did not apply structural theory in his considerations on art, most of his works on the subject having been written before his introduction of the notions of an unconscious ego, id and super-ego. Now the unconscious ego is very much involved in an artist's approach to resolving the conflict that induces him to produce a work, as we shall see, and from this point of view the production of a dream may be likened to that of a work of art.

Freud's classical theory is thus found to include indications that the impact of art works stems both from the artist's repressed wishes, concealed in the form of a work of art, and from his intention to arouse in other people the same emotional attitude that gave rise to his creative impetus – a phenomenon not unlike the processes underlying the formation of a dream.

90

Symbols of different kinds

In her study *Dream, Art, Phantasy*, Segal (1991) concentrates on the part played by symbols of different kinds in the impact of a work of art, suggesting causes for that almost indefinable entity, artistic emotion. Some of her hypotheses may also help us understand the emotional impact of dreams that turn over a page on both dreamer and analyst.

As we know, Segal (1957) distinguishes two forms of symbol formation and the symbolic function, namely the symbolic equation on the one hand and true symbolism or symbolic representation on the other. Transitional forms exist between the two. The true symbol, experienced as the representative of the object, comes into being when depressive feelings outweigh paranoid–schizoid feelings and when separation from the object, ambivalence, guilt and loss can be tolerated.

It follows from the foregoing that the depressive position does not lead solely to the creation of symbolic representations, as might initially be thought, but also to an increased capacity to contain symbolic equations. This widened conception of the depressive position extends the range of possibilities of representations, linking symbolic equations to symbols: in other words, it increases the individual's capacity to integrate and contain more primitive aspects of his experience, including the primitive symbolic equations. It seems to me that this extension of the concept of the depressive position casts light on important aspects of the formation of the dreams I describe, because the working through of the depressive position leads the dreamer not only to produce symbolic representations but also to include primitive aspects of the dream experience in the form of symbolic equations.

Aesthetic impact and symbolism

Applying her views on the different forms of symbols to aesthetic experience, Segal postulates that one factor in the immediate impact of a work of art is the presence of concrete symbolic elements juxtaposed with more mature elements of symbolism, the latter, as we have just seen, being connected with the depressive position:

> Any art, in particular, does embody concrete symbolic elements that give a work of art its immediate 'punch'; it has a concrete impact on our experience provided it is included in an otherwise more evolved type of symbolism, without which it would be no more than a meaningless bombardment.
>
> (Segal 1991: 43)

Unlike dreams, however, art works have the property of 'embodying themselves' in material reality; for this reason, their aesthetic impact depends partly on the way the artist uses the concrete medium to express his fantasies: '[The artist] is not only a dreamer but a supreme artisan. An artisan may not be an artist, but an artist must be an artisan' (ibid.: 96).

Is aesthetic impact 'embodied' in dreams?

If Segal is right in postulating that the immediate impact of a work of art is due to the concrete symbolic elements – materialized by the artist's work as an artisan – how can this be applied to dreams? Do dreams possess an equivalent to these concrete symbolic elements, which might account for the fact that certain dreams have a more immediate impact than others? Dreams, admittedly, are only dreams: they offer fantasy solutions to fantasy problems and, with respect to reality, they possess neither the property of children's play that creates an important link between fantasy and reality, nor the characteristic of an art work that 'embodies' unconscious fantasies through the material reality on which the artist has worked.

However, while a dream is not embodied in concrete reality in the same way as a work of art, it nevertheless has an aesthetic impact of the same kind; hence the question: What is the dream equivalent of what is 'embodied' in art through its symbolic elements? The sense impressions in a dream are on occasion certainly so intense that the dreamer experiences them as reality: *in this case, could the 'embodied' dimension of dreams be attributed to these vivid sensory impressions that accompany certain dreams, and might it have to do with symbolic equations in which bodily reality is hardly, if at all, distinguished from fantasy?* What then tells us that the experience is a dream and not reality? In my view, part of the answer is our capacity to *distinguish between different modalities of symbolism*, acquired by the working through of the depressive position. Furthermore, perhaps it is the juxtaposition of the two modalities of symbolism that enables us to tolerate the madness of psychic reality – on the one hand a primitive symbolism that enables us to 'touch' psychic reality almost concretely by reducing the gap between reality and fantasy (symbolic equation) and, on the other hand, a more evolved symbolism whereby we can simultaneously distinguish and unite virtual reality and material reality, fantasy and concrete reality, or, for that matter, true symbolism and symbolic representation.

The role of reparation in the impetus to create and in dream formation

Another element in the importance of an art work and its impact may be that the artist's unconscious ego is engaged in the search for resolution of a conflict;

92

on this point Segal's works on dreams and on art converge. In her view, dreams perform a number of functions: they are not only the fantasy expression of an unconscious conflict but also the search for a fantasy resolution of this conflict, and the dream work is directly concerned with its working through. The same applies to art, because, if there is wish fulfilment in art, the object is mainly to find a solution to an unconscious problem situation, and not merely to fulfil an unsatisfied omnipotent wish.

However, Segal goes further, taking the view that the crucial factor in the creative impetus is the need for reparation that arises out of the working through of the depressive position. Basing her argument on the link established by Klein (1928) between the need for reparation and the origin of the creative impulse observed in a woman painter, Segal illustrates the relevance of the depressive position, noting in particular the artist's need to recreate what he feels in the depths of his internal world: 'It is his inner perception of the deepest feeling of the depressive position that his internal world is shattered which leads to the necessity for the artist to recreate something that is felt to be a whole new world' (Segal 1991: 86).

If Freud was right in his view that the artist seeks to evoke in the spectator the same constellation of unconscious feelings that motivated him to create his work, we can surely postulate further that the artist seeks to communicate not only his conflict but also his attempt to bring reparation to a resolution. The means of achieving this must then succeed in producing an identification with these processes in others, so that the aesthetic experience involves, for the individual who has it, not only personal psychic work but also the feeling that he must contribute to the process of reparation by identifying with the creator. This process of identification affords him access to deeper feelings than he could attain by himself, as well as making him wish to contribute to the reparative psychic work.

The above views, in my opinion, suggest significant parallels between the factors that underlie, on the one hand, the creative impulse and the means whereby the artist captivates the spectator and, on the other, certain dreams that captivate both the dreamer and the psychoanalyst more than other dreams.

Might dreams – especially dreams that turn over a page – thus result from a need for reparation born of the working through of the depressive position, along the same lines as the origins of the creative impulse? Might we postulate that these dreams, which arise when previously disavowed and split-off components are gathered together and taken back into the ego, have to do with the unconscious memory of a harmonious internal world and with the experience of its destruction and fragmentation – that is, with the depressive position? If so, such dreams would form part of a process aimed at rediscovering this lost internal world in the dreamer's conscious mind, in such a way as to recreate that world in a new way – although the resolution will never be complete, as the work of reparation is never done.

Again, might one of the aims of the dreamer, like the artist in relation to his public, be to try to evoke in the psychoanalyst not only the same constellation of unconscious feelings that motivated him, but also the conflict and the attempt to bring reparation to a resolution? *Can a significant analogy not be drawn, too, between, on the one hand, the identification of a person empathizing with the deep feelings communicated to him by the artist through his work and, on the other, the psychoanalyst's identification with unconscious aspects which his patient projects on to him by telling him his dreams and associating to them – that is, an empathic identification with the patient's conflicts and with the wish to elaborate a resolution communicated to him by his patient?*

Magritte: The obsessive search for a resolution

Before ending, I should like to illustrate the parallel that can be drawn between, on the one hand, the work of an artist as an artisan in search of a resolution of his intrapsychic conflicts through his works intended for the public and, on the other, the psychic work of a dreamer in his relationship with his analyst, which resembles that of the artist in many respects. I have already presented the clinical example of a dream brought by my patient Tania, which provided me with much information about the intrapsychic conflicts she was attempting to resolve by projecting them into the transference relationship.

I shall therefore end by describing a different type of experience, both artistic and to some degree clinical, occasioned by my contact with the works of the painter René Magritte. His friend and critic Torczyner had clearly discerned the extent to which Magritte's artistic work was profoundly inspired by the search for a resolution that impelled him to create ever new forms of painting: 'Magritte sets no store by his art, but the greatest store by the problems it presents to him. They obsess him until he finds solutions to them' (Torczyner 1977: 22).

Although my mind had long been exercised by the bizarre appearance of Magritte's paintings and by his use of symbolism, it was only when I visited a retrospective of his works at the Modern Art Museum in the Centre Beaubourg, Paris, some years ago that I discovered a significant unifying theme in them. Confronted with the large number of canvases on show, I re-experienced the sense of strangeness that both his paintings and his drawings had always inspired in me; in them, Magritte seeks to convey an enigmatic message which, while cast in ever new forms, nevertheless seems to recur like an elusive but fascinating leitmotif.

I first viewed the pictures in the chronological order in which they were hung, and then returned to the starting point to read the biographical details displayed in the exhibition rooms. I stopped in my tracks at one of these panels, which told me that Magritte's mother had drowned herself while suffering from acute schizophrenia when her son was 14 years old. I was both overwhelmed and enlightened to learn of this episode, of which I had previously been unaware, and toured the exhibition again, looking at each picture in chronological order, with this tragic event constantly in mind. This new insight confirmed my idea of a unifying thread running through the whole of this great artist's oeuvre, which could be seen as a constantly renewed attempt not only to work through his mourning for his mother, but also to bring reparation to a resolution by way of the creative impulse that impelled him to paint.

For this purpose, Magritte made large-scale use of the different forms of symbolism with a view to conveying and arousing emotion through the transformations he imposed on visual representations. For example, I realized that Magritte would often juxtapose the two forms of symbolization – symbolic representation and the symbolic equation – in order to evoke in others the traumatic shock he had experienced upon the sudden loss of his mother. This feeling links up with the universal sense of irremediable loss that is the lot of every individual when confronted with the separation from and loss of the first object. Magritte was to express it throughout his oeuvre in myriad different ways, through the recurring medium of violent contrasts – between life and death, animate and inanimate, vegetation and stone, a human figure or object suspended in space and the sensation of an imminent fall, and so on. One of Magritte's favourite subjects is the representation of a woman or part of a woman in the form of a female body, bust or face, whose living outline, however, contrasts with the cold marble of a statue, evoking the idea of death and the grave. This artist often arouses an uncanny feeling or a sense of weirdness or anxiety through a cut-out silhouette of a figure that is then hollowed out, suggesting absence, separation or death. Magritte was also capable of conveying the depressive feeling that gripped him throughout his life, with its ups and downs and obsessions, at the same time communicating to the spectator the feelings and sensations that possessed him. I am thinking in particular of one picture that shows a giant apple almost filling the entire space in the middle of a room, giving rise to a sense of suffocation – just as the introjected lost object may, in melancholic depression, be felt to invade and merge with the ego to the point of asphyxiating it. On occasion, in connection with a happy relationship with a woman, the painter succeeds in communicating a sense of peace and serenity, as in the famous series of silhouettes depicting a night-black house standing out against a bright daytime sky.

While each Magritte painting, considered by itself, can be seen as a snapshot of the emotion that is in my view closely bound up with the traumatic event mentioned earlier, when we come to consider his oeuvre as a whole in its chronological continuity we obtain a perspective view of the artist's attempt to work through the mourning associated with his mother's death – an aim in which he does indeed partly succeed. Whereas most of his paintings, drawings and sketches reflect one aspect or another of this crucial mourning work, they do not all do so in the same way, or with the same intensity, so that, from this point of view, some of the pictures are more significant than others. Again, even if some of Magritte's works tend more to convey his anxiety and depression, so that they have a powerful impact on the spectator, this does not mean that the primitive symbolic representations in them are more expressive of the severity of the artist's suffering, let alone that they reveal a niche of encapsulated madness. On the contrary, some of his most pregnant productions demonstrate the talent of an accomplished artist who has succeeded in extending the scope of pictorial representation and allowing his most dramatic conflicts to coexist with moments of peace and serenity in one and the same work – just as aggression and destruction, in Magritte, are bedfellows of a zest for life.

Magritte thus seemed to me to be one of the painters who best illustrated the idea, present in every work of art, that the artist seeks not only to evoke in the spectator the same constellation of unconscious feelings that have motivated his impetus to create, as Freud believed, but also to bring the process of reparation to a successful conclusion through the spectator's identification with the artist. In Segal's view, this process of identification is one of the main determinants of aesthetic emotion:

> And if I am right in thinking that the specific constellation that is aimed at in depth has to do with an attempted resolution of a depressive conflict, including its early Oedipal constellation, then the means must be such as to convey both the conflict and the reparative attempt at resolution.
>
> (Segal 1991: 89)

Through his creative impetus, the painter – like the dreamer – thus finds a temporary outlet for his need for reparation, in the knowledge that this process will never be completed and must be constantly renewed.

Conclusions

The year 2000 witnessed a renewal of psychoanalytic interest in dreams, coinciding with the centenary of Freud's publication of *The Interpretation of Dreams* in 1900. This revival is welcome.

Although clinical discussions show that dream interpretation retains an important position in the daily work of psychoanalysts with their analysands, the fact is that it is no longer predominant. A progressive disaffection with the theoretical study of dreams in psychoanalysis has come about in the last few decades. This is indicated by the relative dearth of publications on the subject, particularly in the French language, even though many published psychoanalytic case histories are still illustrated by a dream.

Why this partial disaffection? In my view, there are three main reasons. The first has to do with the growing importance assigned since the 1950s to transference interpretation, of which the interpretation of dreams is regarded as a particular case, as Flanders (1993) points out. The second is presumably that many psychoanalysts today still approach their analysands' dreams from the point of view of repression. Yet we are increasingly confronted with patients who deploy not only neurotic but also primitive defence mechanisms such as disavowal, splitting and projective identification, in which the function of dreaming is disturbed. For this reason, where the dream function is deficient, it is important to interpret the function performed by the dream in the session before tackling the content. According to Segal (1991), the pessimism sometimes expressed about the usefulness of dreams results from the fact that their interpretation is still approached along primarily classical lines today.

Besides these two reasons for the loss of interest in dreams, I believe there is also a third. It is the fascination of some psychoanalysts with recent neuroscientific discoveries about brain function. So far, however, our knowledge has not progressed far enough – in particular, where dreams are concerned – to draw meaningful parallels between the neuroscientific and psychoanalytic fields without running the risk of confusion.

Now as in the past, psychoanalysis proceeds by an essentially personal and internal approach, constantly fuelled by clinical experience, and, to a greater extent than other disciplines, involves a perpetual alternation between theory and technique. This has been my own attitude since my very first observations on dreams that turn over a page. I began by considering them in terms of classical theory, but my ideas subsequently evolved until I was able to accommodate these dreams within a broadened contemporary conception of psychic functioning that allows for the vicissitudes of the integration of splits. I invite the reader of this book to do likewise.

Bibliography

Anzieu, D. (1988) Préface. In: *'Sur les rêves' de Freud, S., 1901*, Paris: Gallimard.

Arieti, S. (1963) 'The psychotherapy of schizophrenia in theory and practice', *Psychiatric Research Report No. 17*, Washington: American Psychiatric Association.

Bion, W.R. (1957) 'Differentiation of the psychotic from the non-psychotic personalities', *International Journal of Psycho-Analysis*, 38: 266–275. [Also in *Second Thoughts*, New York: Jason Aronson, 1977.]

—— (1962) *Learning from Experience*, London: Heinemann.

—— (1992) *Cogitations*, London: Karnac.

Blechner, M.J. (1983) 'Changes in the dreams of borderline patients', *Contemporary Psychoanalysis*, 19: 485–498.

—— (2000) Letter to the Editor on J.M. Quinodoz' 'Dreams that turn over a page', *International Journal of Psycho-Analysis*, 81: 174.

Bourguignon, A., Cotet, P., Laplanche, J., and Robert, F. (1989) *Traduire Freud*, Paris: Presses Universitaires de France.

Britton, R. (1998) *Belief and Imagination*, London and New York: Routledge.

Capozzi, P., and De Masi, F. (2001) 'The meaning of dreams in the psychotic state', *International Journal of Psycho-Analysis*, 82: 933–952.

Fain, M., and David, C. (1963) 'Aspects fonctionnels de la vie onirique. Rapport de Congrès', *Revue française de psychanalyse*, 27: 241–343.

Ferenczi, S. (1931) 'On the revision of the Interpretation of Dreams', Notes and fragments, in *Final Contributions to Psycho-Analysis*, London: Hogarth, 1980.

Ferro, A. (2000) 'Sexuality as a narrative genre or dialect in the consulting-room: a radical vertex', in *W.R. Bion Between Past and Future*, P. Bion Talamo, F. Borgogno and S. Merciai (eds), London and New York: Karnac.

Flanders, S. (1993) *The Dream Discourse Today*, London and New York: Routledge.

Freud, S. (1900a) *The Interpretation of Dreams*, SE 4–5.

—— (1901a) 'Sur les rêves', Paris: Gallimard, 1988 [French version of 'On dreams', SE 5].

—— (1910d) 'The future prospects of psycho-analytic therapy', SE 11.

—— (1914b) 'The Moses of Michelangelo', SE 13.

—— (1914g) 'Remembering, repeating and working-through', SE 12.

—— (1915) Papers on metapsychology, SE 14.

—— (1919h) 'The "uncanny"', SE 17.

—— (1923b) *The Ego and the Id*, SE 19.

—— (1924e) 'The loss of reality in neurosis and psychosis', SE 19.

—— (1926d [1925]) *Inhibitions, Symptoms and Anxiety*, SE 20.

—— (1933a [1932]) *New Introductory Lectures on Psycho-Analysis*, SE 22.

—— (1940a [1938]) *An Outline of Psycho-Analyis*, SE 23.

Garma, A. (1970) *Psychoanalysis of Dreams*, New York: Jason Aronson, 1974.

Grinberg, L. (1962) 'On a specific aspect of countertransference due to the patient's projective identification', *International Journal of Psycho-Analysis*, 43: 2.

—— (1967) 'Función del soñar y clasificación clínica de los sueños en el proceso analítico', *Revista de Psicoanálisis*, 24: 749–789.

—— (1979) 'Countertransference and projective identification', in *Countertransference*, L. Epstein and A.H. Feiner (eds), New York: Jason Aronson.

—— (1987) 'Dreams and acting out', *Psychoanalytic Quarterly*, 56: 155–176.

Grubrich-Simitis, I. (2000), 'Metamorphoses of *The Interpretation of Dreams*: Freud's conflicted relations with his book of the century', *International Journal of Psycho-Analysis*, 81: 1155–1184.

Guillaumin, J. (1979) *Le rêve et le Moi*, Paris: Presses Universitaires de France.

Hinshelwood, R.D. (1989) *A Dictionary of Kleinian Thought*, London: Free Association Books.

—— (2000) Introduction, in *Dictionnaire de la pensée kleinienne* [French translation by G. Nagler of *A Dictionary of Kleinian Thought*], Paris: Presses Universitaires de France.

Isaacs, S. (1948) 'The nature and function of phantasy', in *Developments in Psycho-Analysis*, London: Hogarth, 1989.

Khan, M.R. (1962) 'Dream psychology and the evolution of the psychoanalytic situation', in S. Flanders, ed., *The Dream Discourse Today*, London and New York: Routledge, 1993.

Klein, M. (1928) 'Early stages of the Oedipus conflict', in *The Writings of Melanie Klein*, Volume I, 1921–1945, London: Karnac, 1992.

—— (1934) 'A contribution to the psychogenesis of manic-depressive states', in *The Writings of Melanie Klein*, Vol. I, 1921–1945, London: Karnac, 1992.

—— (1940) 'Mourning and its relation to manic-depressive states', in *The Writings of Melanie Klein*, Vol. I, 1921–1945, London: Karnac, 1992.

Lansky, M.R. (1992) *Essential Papers on Dreams*, New York and London: New York University Press.

Laplanche, J., and Pontalis, J.-B. (1967) *The Language of Psycho-Analysis*, London: Hogarth, 1973.

Lewin, B.D. (1946) 'Sleep, the mouth, and the dream screen', *Psychoanalytic Quarterly*, 15: 419–434.

Mahler, M., Pine, F., and Bergman, A. (1975) *The Psychological Birth of the Human Infant*, New York: Basic Books, 1991.

Meltzer, D. (1984) *Dream Life: A Re-Examination of the Psycho-Analytical Theory and Technique*, Perthshire: Clunie Press, 1983.

O'Shaughnessy, E. (2000), 'Dreaming and not dreaming', *Bulletin of the British Psycho-Analytical Society*, November 2000, 36: 28–33.

Perelberg, R. (ed.) (2000) *Dreaming and Thinking*, London: Institute of Psycho-Analysis.

Perron-Borelli, M., and Perron, R. (1987) 'Fantasme et action', *Revue française de psychanalyse*, 51: 539–636.

Quinodoz, D. (1984) 'L'incapacité de bien traiter ses objets internes comme expression de l'homosexualité latente', *Revue française de psychanalyse*, 48: 745–750.
—— (1992) 'The psychoanalytic setting as the instrument of the container function', *International Journal of Psycho-Analysis*, 73: 627–635.
—— (1994a) 'Interpretations in projection', *International Journal of Psycho-Analysis*, 75: 755–761.
—— (1994b) *Emotional Vertigo: Between Anxiety and Pleasure*, trans. A. Pomerans, London and New York: Routledge, 1997.
Quinodoz, J.-M. (1987) 'Des "rêves qui tournent la page"', *Revue française de psychanalyse*, 51: 837–838.
—— (1989) 'Female homosexual patients in psychoanalysis', *International Journal of Psycho-Analysis*, 70: 55–63.
—— (1991) *The Taming of Solitude: Separation Anxiety in Psychoanalysis*, trans. P. Slotkin, London and New York: Routledge, 1993.
—— (1999) '"Dreams that turn over a page": integration dreams with paradoxical regressive content', *International Journal of Psycho-Analysis*, 80: 225–238.
—— (2000a) Response to Mark J. Blechner's Letter to the Editor on 'Dreams that turn over a page', *International Journal of Psycho-Analysis*, 81: 175.
—— (2000b) 'Rêves d'intégration à contenu paradoxal régressif: les "rêves qui tournent une page"', *Revue française de psychanalyse*, 64: 1121–1135.
—— (2000c) 'Mélancolie maniaque: quelle issue?', *Revue française de psychanalyse*, 64: 1825–1835.
—— (2000d) 'Discussion of "Dreaming and not dreaming" by Ms Edna O'Shaughnessy', *Bulletin of the British Psycho-Analytical Society*, November 2000, 36: 7, 34.
Rosenfeld, H. (1987) *Impasse and Interpretation*, London and New York: Routledge.
Rycroft, C. (1951) 'A contribution to the study of the dream screen', in *Imagination and Reality*, London: Hogarth, 1968.
Segal, H. (1952) 'A psychoanalytic approach to aesthetics', in *The Work of Hanna Segal*, New York: Jason Aronson, 1981.
—— (1957) 'Notes on symbol formation', in *The Work of Hanna Segal*, New York: Jason Aronson, 1981.
—— (1964) *Introduction to the Work of Melanie Klein*, London: Hogarth, 1978.
—— (1973) 'The functions of dreams', in *The Work of Hanna Segal*, New York: Jason Aronson, 1981.
—— (1988), 'Sweating it out', *The Psychoanalytic Study of the Child*, 43: 167–175.
—— (1991) *Dream, Art, Phantasy*, London and New York: Routledge.
Sharpe, E.F. (1937) *Dream Analysis*, London: Hogarth, 1978.
Stewart, H. (1973) 'The experiencing of the dream and the transference', *International Journal of Psycho-Analysis*, 54: 345–347.
—— (1981) 'The technical use, and experiencing, of dreams', *International Journal of Psycho-Analysis*, 62: 301–307.
—— (1992) *Psychic Experience and Problems of Technique*, London and New York: Routledge.
Torczyner, H. (1977) *René Magritte*, Paris: Draeger.
Williams, P. (1999) Internet discussion review: '"Dreams that turn over a page": integration dreams with paradoxical regressive content' by Jean-Michel Quinodoz, *International Journal of Psycho-Analysis*, 80: 845–856.

Winnicott, D.W. (1947) 'Hate in the counter-transference', in *Collected Papers: Through Paediatrics to Psychoanalysis*, London: Tavistock, 1958.

Author index

Anzieu, D. 70
Arieti, S. 55, 59–60, 78

Bion, W. R. xiv, 12, 13, 16, 57, 75–6, 77, 78, 86, 89
Blechner, M. J. 55, 60–1, 78
Bourguignon, A., Cottet, P., Laplanche, J. and Robert, F. 11
Britton, R. xiv

Capozzi, P. and de Masi, F. 86

Diatkine, R. 23

Fain, M. and David, C. 71
Ferenczi, S. 55, 58
Ferro, A. 35
Flanders, S. 21, 71, 97
Freud, S. 3, 11, 12, 13, 20, 25, 26, 55, 56–7, 69–71, 80, 90, 93, 96

Garma, A. 58
Grinberg, L. 13, 15, 55, 61, 74
Grubrich-Simitis, I. 70
Guillaumin, J. 28, 55, 64–5, 71

Hering, C. 25
Hinshelwood, R. D. 74

Isaacs, S. 26
Israël, P. 42

Khan, M. R. 67
Klein, M. xiv, 26, 27, 28, 44, 57, 74, 80, 93

Lacan, J. 57
Lansky, M. R. 70
Laplanche, J. and Pontalis, J. B. 11
Lewin, B. D. 67

Magritte, R. 94–6
Mahler, M., Pine, F. and Bergman, A. 23
Meltzer, D. 75

O'Shaughnessy, E. 26, 29, 39, 84–6

Ponsi, M. 20
Perelberg, R. 71
Perron-Borelli, M. and Perron, R. 4

Quinodoz, D. 8, 16, 36, 44
Quinodoz, J. M. xiii–xiv, 3, 4, 7, 8, 12, 16, 21, 22, 35, 55, 57, 61, 79, 81, 85

Rosenfeld, H. 29, 84–5, 86
Rycroft, C. 67

Segal, H. xiii–xiv, 8, 13, 27, 28, 33, 36, 38, 39, 43, 55, 62–4, 67, 75, 78, 81, 90–3, 96–7
Sharpe, E. F. 21
Stewart, H. 13, 55, 65–8

Torczyner, H. 94

Williams, P. 7, 20, 55
Winnicott, D. W. 55, 58–9

Subject index

aggression: 9, 14, 24, 51; and destructiveness 15, 24, 51, 52; destructive superego 86; link between love and hate 23, 24, 34–5, 51–2; and transference 18, 24, 38, 46
ambivalence: 5, 10, 15, 22, 24, 24–5, 40–1, 42, 47, 52, 86
anxiety: 9–13, 61, 62–4, 74, 80, 84; capacity to tolerate 16; castration 5, 43, 50; claustrophobic 5, 9; dissipation of 10, 34; dreams of anxiety in Freud 56; Freud's theories of 13, 80; separation anxiety and object loss 7, 21–2, 63, 81; and symbolization 38–9; and threat to the ego's cohesion 56–7, 80–1
art: aesthetic impact of dreams that turn over a page 89–94; aesthetic pleasure in Freud 90; search for a resolution in Magritte's painting 94–6

bisexuality: psychic 18, 24, 29, 85
borderline: 60–1, 73, 78, 89
buoyancy: xiii, 79, 81

clinical examples: 4–6, 14–15, 16–19, 24–5, 40–52, 59–60, 62, 64, 71–3, 82, 84–5, 85
containing capacity: 14–19, 36, 88; and capacity for reverie 16; expulsion of 36; identification with the analyst's 16, 18–19, 36–7, 81–3
content (dream): latent 9, 33, 38, 69, 72–3; manifest 9, 10, 38, 67, 69, 72–3

counter transference: 14–19, 36, 59, 63, 87–8; and containing capacity 14–19; and projective counteridentification 15; risk of yielding to the dreamer's anxiety 14–15, 62–3

defences: and dreams 48, 59–60, 72, 73; mechanisms of 27–8, 29, 51, 57, 60, 63,78; primitive and neurotic 42, 56, 63, 65, 78, 82–3, 89
depressive position: xiii–xiv, 12–13, 22–3, 34, 39, 61, 73, 74, 79, 89, 91; link between love and hate 24–5, 34, 51–2; PS – D oscillation xiii–xiv, 73, 77–8; and reparation 92–3
disavowal: 29, 37; impact of the disavowed 88–9; 'return' of the disavowed 11–12, 26, 47, 79, 88
dream, dreams: of anxiety and termination of analysis 14, 62–4; in borderline 60–1, 78; clinical and aesthetic impact 87–9; container 67; curative 58–9; of departure 58–9, 81; ego's overwhelming 13, 65–8; elaborative 61; evacuative 61; fulfilment of an unsatisfied unconscious wish 33, 56, 69; life and death drives 70, 82–3, 86; mechanisms of 69; mixed 61; and neurosciences 69, 97; negative therapeutic reaction 25, 84–5; recapitulative 28, 64–5; search for a resolution 39, 59–60; 75; screen 67; space 67; and transference 21; traumatic 58; *see also* clinical

examples, dreams that turn over a page, dream work, function performed by the dream

'dreams that turn over a page': characteristics 3–4, 6, 9–30; clarity and coherence 26–9, 46–7, 64–5, 85, 87; clinical and aesthetic impact 87–9; and analyst's containing capacity 14–19, 36; and countertransference 14–19; interpretation in two stages 18–19, 30–9; metaphor 8; and negative therapeutic reaction 25, 84–5; and nightmare 10, 62; paradoxical character 3, 6, 20; and preliminary interviews 89; and retreat in response to progress 23; retrospective illumination 26–9, 50–1; and separation anxiety 8, 21–2, 81; and transference 21; *see also* clinical examples

dream work: 69, 74–6, 82–3, 86; deficiency in 35–6; dream-work-α 13, 75, 86

drive: life and death drives 70, 82–3, 86

ego: 56, 65, 70; capacity to repress 73, cohesion 12, 37, 72, 73, 74, 78–81, 83; ego-overwhelming dreams 13, 55, 65–8; fragmentation 34–5, 58, 80; recasting 77–8; splitting of 74, 79–80;

enactment: 43–4, 78, 85

fantasy: unconscious 26–8, 38, 65, 73, 85

function of the dream: deficiency 37, 97; interpretation 35–6, 38; performed by the dream 35–6, 37, 39, 74–5

hallucinations: 59–60, 62, 64

hate: link between love and hate 23, 24, 34–6, 49, 51–2

heterosexual (tendencies): 18, 24, 28–9, 43, 48–9, 52, 88

homosexual (tendencies): 17–19, 24, 28–9, 35, 48–9, 52, 88

identification: to the analyst's containing capacity 16, 18–19, 36–7, 38, 83; and psychic bisexuality 18, 24, 29, 85

impact: aesthetic 89–96; clinical 87–9

integration (psychic), 7, 12, 21–3, 34–6, 61, 64, 74–82, 82–3, 86;

interpretation: 6, 34, 59; of the function performed by the dream 35–6; unsaturated 35; in projection 36–7; in two stages 10, 18–19, 33–9

introjection: 22, 28, 83; of a good object 63, 81

latent: content 9, 33, 38, 69, 72–3

love: 52; link between love and hate 23, 24, 35–6, 51–2; link between love and genital sexuality 48–9, 51–2

madness: fear of 9, 13, 17, 25, 38, 45, 62, 66, 80

manifest: content 9, 38, 67, 69, 72

mourning: 38, 82, 95

negative therapeutic reaction: 25, 84–5

neurosis: 12, 38, 56, 78; and psychosis 12, 57, 60–1, 78

nightmare: 10, 62

object relations: 21–2, 24, 27, 51–2, 61, 63, 71, 80, 83; and narcissism 5–6, 58; perception of the analyst as a separate and different object 5–6, 13, 37–8, 65, 66

Oedipus complex: direct 17, 43; and feminine identification 44, 45, 71–3; and incestuous wishes 52, 72, 88; reversed 19, 43, 47, 52

paranoid-schizoid position: xiii–xiv, 12–13, 22–3, 39, 63, 73, 74, 77–8; and integration 74; PS – D oscillation xiii–xiv, 73, 77–8

personality structure: 27–8, 87–8

preliminary interviews: 89

progress: 6, 14, 20–5, 60, 65–6, 79; criteria 22–3, 36, 62–4; and negative therapeutic reaction 25, 84–5; retreat in response to progress 20–5, 35, 47–8, 84–5

projection: 'return' of split-off and projected parts of the self 11–13, 22–3, 27–8, 41, 58, 62; withdrawal 12

projective counteridentification: 15

projective identification: 22, 38, 42, 45, 58, 62–3, 66, 67, 72, 74, 76, 89 psychosis: 12, 13, 56–7, 59–60, 62–4, 73, 74, 75–6; and neurosis 12, 56–7, 60–1, 78

regression: in response to progress 6, 14–5, 20–5
reparation: 24, 39, 50, 75, 86, 91, 92–3
representation: symbolic 25, 28–9, 38–9, 44–5, 66, 71–3, 74–5, 81
repression, repressed: 11–12, 34, 37, 51, 56, 73, 90; distinct from splitting 34, 37, 88–9; impact of 88–9; reappearance of the repressed 51–2; 'return' of the repressed 11–12, 26, 29, 56, 79; and splitting 11–12, 29, 34, 81
resolution of a conflict (search for a): 39, 75, 82–9, 92–4; in art 92–4, 94–6; in Magritte's painting 94–6
retrospective illumination: 4, 26–9, 40, 50–1, 59, 66
'return': of the repressed and disavowed 12–13, 29, 56–7, 79; of split-off and projected parts of the self 11–13, 29, 79–80, 81, 83

separation: separation anxiety and object loss 7, 21–2, 63, 81, 82, 91; separateness 67
sexuality: 18–19, 48–9, 88; castration anxiety 5, 43, 50; and dream 58, 71–3; masculine identification in the girl 47, 49; and identification with the genital mother 44, 45, 49–50, 71–3; link between love and genital sexuality 48–9, 51–2; sadistic primal scene 49: *see also* bisexuality (psychic), heterosexual tendencies, homosexual tendencies
solitude (sense of): 22, 23

splitting, splits: 29, 37; difference between Freud and Klein 74; different types of 74; of the ego 74, 79–80; of the ego in neurosis and psychosis 57, 66, 78; impact of 88–9; gathering together of split-off parts of the self 7, 77, 79–80, 81–2; and integration 26, 29, 81, 97; replaced by repression 51, 65, 66, 81; and repression 11–12, 16, 29, 34, 37–8, 88–9, 99; 'return' of split-off parts of the self 11–13, 29, 79–80
superego: 70, 74, 76, 83–4, 90; destructive 86
symbol, symbolization, symbolism: aesthetic impact 91–2; and depressive position 39, 73, 85; and reparation 39, 91; symbolic equation 38–9, 91; symbolic representation 25, 28–9, 38–9, 44–5, 66, 71–3, 74–5, 81, 91

termination: of analysis 5, 14–15, 62–4, 78, 82; and dreams of anxiety 14, 62–4
theory of dreams: classical 7, 21, 37, 60, 69–71, 83, 93; post-Freudian 7–8, 21, 69–71, 93
transference: 5, 12, 14–19, 21, 26, 40–52, 70, 73, 96; dreams and 21; identification with the analyst's containing capacity 16, 18–19, 37, 38, 82; as a total situation 33
trauma, traumatic: dreams 58

uncanny (*unheimlich*): 9–13, 24, 80
unconscious: 12–13, 15, 22, 26–9, 40, 64, 75–6, 89; structure 26

wish (fulfilment of an unsatisfied unconscious): 33, 56, 69